I want chocolate!

*Victoire, this one is for you…*

Trish Deseine

# I want chocolate!

Photography by Marie-Pierre Morel

LAUREL
GLEN

San Diego, California

Chocolate is wonderful, whether it comes in the form of a cake, mousse, drink, or bar. Hot, warm, cold, or frozen, you can't beat it. What other ingredient creates as many culinary opportunities just by being melted?

Chocolate is everywhere—the color is even in the fabrics and materials used by fashion and interior designers—but it's especially in our food, both sweet and savory. Next, we'll be plastering ourselves with chocolate to nourish our starved skin and to smooth wrinkles! It doesn't matter where you are, you can learn about its origins, its history, its manufacture, and its benefits.

Faced with this very trendy craze, I wanted to put chocolate back to what, in my mind, is its rightful place—somewhere between sensuality, nostalgia, emotion, and sheer greed.

That is why this book is divided into chapters that correspond to each moment in our lives and that reflect why we really want chocolate. We would never make a chocolate-spread sandwich for dinner guests, nor would we ever spend half a day making a fancy cake in the event of an attack of the blues, when what we really need is a quick nibble of a square or two of chocolate.

You will find that all the recipes and ideas contained in this book are really very easy to make. If a self-taught, lazy, impatient, and disorganized cook like me can manage it, it will be a piece of cake for you!

So without further ado, munch your way through my book!

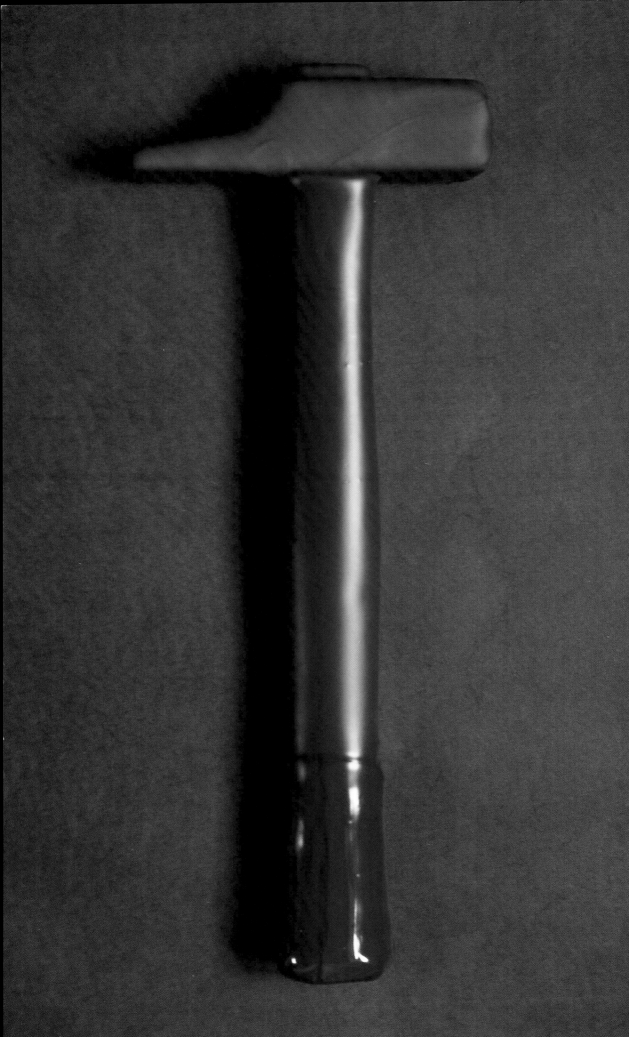

# Chocolate
# tool kit

# A few tips before we begin

Now that you have a book on chocolate, it's worthwhile doing things by the book!

1 Insist on using good quality chocolate. If you are buying chocolate from supermarkets, don't settle for bottom-of-the-range products; buy the best. Check out the Swiss bittersweet varieties, which can be found in some supermarkets or specialty stores. Unsweetened baking chocolate is very bitter and is used primarily in baking. Plain semisweet and bittersweet chocolate candy bars are excellent melted for desserts and cakes and are also available in chocolate chip form. White chocolate can also be bought as white baking chips. Cocoa powder has the cocoa butter removed before being processed into ground powder. Do not use cocoa drink mixes instead of cocoa powder as these have added milk powder and sugar that will alter the flavor of your chosen recipe.

But I can tell you now that that chocolate will not melt as well, will never have the same complexity, the same quality of flavors as a *couverture*

chocolate bought from a chocolate-maker or confectioner, in a gourmet food store, or from a supplier to the professionals.

2 Don't succumb to the current snobbery about the percentage of cocoa solids in the chocolate. A chocolate won't be any better for your cake just because it contains eighty percent cocoa solids rather than sixty-four percent. Quite the contrary in fact, because the latter will definitely blend better with the other ingredients. Always follow your own personal preferences.

3 Stop thinking of milk chocolate and white chocolate as inferior products—they can be excellent. They are delicious ingredients to create mixtures and marriages that are just as sophisticated as those made with dark chocolate.

4 In this book, I try not to give too many pointless details or intimidating explanations, but it is very important to observe the comments that are made below.

**Softened butter** It is important that the butter does not melt completely. This is essential if it is to be beaten with sugar or eggs. Leave the butter to soften at room temperature. Do not put it in a microwave or on a hot surface.

**Flour** I use all-purpose flour. Always sift it (along with the baking powder and cocoa powder, if used in the recipe).

**Cocoa powder** Unsweetened and good quality. It's best sifted.

**Eggs** Medium. Leave the whites to come to room temperature before whisking them. A few recipes include raw eggs. It is advisable not to serve those dishes to very young children, pregnant women, elderly people, or anyone weakened by serious illness. Be sure that the eggs you use are as fresh as possible. If in any doubt, consult your doctor.

### Grease/flour/line the baking pan or mold
It is advisable to do so if it is stated in the recipe. Decide not to at your own peril!

**Light and whipping cream** Always use fresh cream and milk to give you the best flavor.

**Baking pan or mold size** This can change everything. Try to use the size indicated. If you try an experiment and it works, let me know!

**Melting chocolate** Break the chocolate into small pieces and place in a bowl over a saucepan containing about two inches of barely simmering water over a low heat and leave until melted. Remove from the heat and stir well. It is important that the water does not touch the bottom of the bowl. Do not be tempted to hurry the process or the chocolate will "seize" into a fudge-like consistency.

**Melt in a microwave oven** I am lucky enough to be able to use couverture chocolate, which melts very easily in a microwave oven. As a fundamental rule, stop the oven frequently and stir the mixture well as you go along, especially when you have to melt butter and/or cream with the chocolate.

If you are not using couverture chocolate, it is advisable to test it beforehand in a microwave or to melt it in a bowl over hot water as described above, especially if it is to be used for coating or in molds. Again, be careful with the water: Do not let it boil, as it will ruin the chocolate, and do not allow the steam to blemish the chocolate. Never add water or fat when melting chocolate unless the recipe calls for it.

### Cooking times and temperatures
These are only indications. Always keep an eye on your dishes as they cook. Reduce the heat by about 50°F if using a convection oven.

# The Best Brownies

One of America's best-known and most popular desserts. Forget the store-bought mixes once and for all, and make your own with real chocolate.

**Makes about 10 brownies**
**Preparation time: 10 minutes**
**Cooking time: 30 minutes**

1 8-inch-square baking pan

6 tablespoons unsalted butter
4 ounces baking chocolate
2 eggs, beaten
1 cup sugar
¾ cup all-purpose flour
½ cup hazelnuts or macadamia nuts, toasted and crushed, or crushed pecans

Preheat the oven to 350°F.

Grease the baking pan.

Melt the butter and chocolate in a microwave or in a bowl over hot water and allow to cool slightly. Add the beaten eggs, followed by the sugar and flour. Mix together quickly but gently, then incorporate the hazelnuts. Pour into the baking pan and bake for about 30 minutes. It should be crisp on top and soft inside.

Allow to cool slightly before turning out and cutting into squares.

Serve while still warm with vanilla ice cream or whipped cream.

TIP • You can also dress up brownies for dessert by cutting out disk shapes with a cookie cutter. Place a scoop of ice cream on the brownie, cover with Chocolate Sauce (see page 18), and serve.

# Light and Airy Cake

The recipe for this extremely light sponge cake comes from my childhood in Ireland and is very popular with my own children.

**Serves 8**
**Preparation time: 5 minutes**
**Cooking time: 25 minutes**

1 handheld electric mixer
2 shallow cake pans, 8 inches in diameter

1 cup unsalted butter or margarine, softened
1 cup sugar
4 eggs
2 cups all-purpose flour
¼ cup cocoa powder, combined with
¼ cup hot water
2 teaspoons baking powder

Preheat the oven to 350°F.

Grease and flour the cake pans.

Place all the ingredients in a large mixing bowl and beat with the electric mixer to form a smooth dough. Transfer the mixture to the baking pans and bake for 25 minutes. The top of the cakes should be soft to the touch. Remove from the oven, allow to cool for a few minutes, then turn out onto a wire rack.

Decorate with whipped cream or, as in Ireland, with Butter Cream (see page 16).

## Variations

To make a coffee sponge cake, omit the cocoa and water mixture and dissolve 2 tablespoons of instant coffee in the beaten eggs before adding them to the rest of the mixture. Decorate with a chocolate cream or Butter Cream frosting.

To make a plain sponge cake, omit the cocoa and water. Decorate with a chocolate cream or Butter Cream frosting.

*Sept/12*
*Liz, Frank.*
*Paula E*
*simple dark*
*chocolate*
*gaze*

# Dark Chocolate and Almond Cake

**Serves 8**
**Preparation time: 10 minutes**
**Cooking time: 50 minutes**
**Best made a day in advance, if possible**

1 food processor
1 deep baking pan, 8 inches in diameter

½ cup unsalted butter, softened
7 ounces semisweet or bittersweet chocolate, chopped into small pieces
5 eggs, separated
¾ cup sugar
1 cup ground almonds
1 teaspoon baking powder
⅔ cup all-purpose flour

Grease and flour the baking pan.

Preheat the oven to 350°F.

Melt the butter and chocolate in a microwave oven or in a bowl over hot water. Remove from the heat and add the egg yolks, then the sugar. Transfer this mixture to the food processor, then add the almonds, baking powder, and flour.

Whisk the egg whites into stiff peaks and, using a wooden spoon, incorporate them gently, a third at a time, into the chocolate mixture. Spoon the mixture into the baking pan and bake for about 50 minutes. The cake is done when it is soft to the touch in the center. Allow to cool for a few minutes in the pan, then turn out onto a wire rack to cool completely.

*check at 35 and on. 50 mins too long*

TIP • As with most cakes made with dark chocolate, it is best to wrap this up and wait until the next day before eating it. It will be all the better for it! Serve with one or more of the "kit" ideas on pages 16 and 18.

# Nathalie's Melt-in-Your-Mouth Chocolate Cake

As a result of the many enthusiastic responses inspired by this recipe (some of them even volunteered by famous pastry chefs), it has become one of my favorites. Remember to make this cake the evening before to serve the next day, or in the morning for the evening if you are entertaining over the weekend.

**Serves 6–8**
**Preparation time: 5 minutes**
**Cooking time: 22 minutes**
**Best made the evening before, if possible**

1 deep baking pan, 8 inches square

**7 ounces best-quality dark chocolate**
**14 tablespoons (1¾ sticks) unsalted butter**
**1¼ cups sugar**
**5 eggs**
**1 tablespoon all-purpose flour**

Preheat the oven to 375°F.

Melt the chocolate and butter in a microwave oven or in a bowl over hot water. Add the sugar and allow to cool slightly. Incorporate the eggs one by one, stirring well with a wooden spoon after adding each. Finally, add the flour and stir until incorporated.

Transfer to the baking pan and bake for 22 minutes. The cake should not quite have set in the middle.

Remove from the oven, turn out quickly, and leave to cool and rest.

SUGGESTION • Serve with one or more of the "kit" ideas on pages 24 and 26.

# Ultrarich Cake–No Flour, No Mixer

The only tools you need to make this rich, sumptuous cake are a medium mixing bowl, a large mixing bowl, a fork, and a baking pan!

**Serves 8–10**
**Preparation time: 15 minutes**
**Cooking time: 45 minutes**
**Best made the evening before, if possible**

1 baking pan, 9 inches in diameter

**2 cups unsalted butter**
**1½ cups whipping cream**
**15 ounces best-quality dark chocolate**
**¾ cup sugar**
**8 eggs**

Preheat the oven to 350°F.

Grease the baking pan. Melt the butter, cream, and chocolate in a microwave oven or in a bowl over hot water. Add the sugar and stir well until dissolved. In a large bowl, beat the eggs with a whisk or fork, then add to the chocolate mixture. Stir well until the mixture is smooth.

Pour into the baking pan and bake for about 40 minutes. Remove from the oven, place on a wire rack, and allow to cool in the pan. When the cake is cool, turn it out and wrap it up well before leaving it to rest overnight in a refrigerator. You can frost it or decorate it with a sprinkling of cocoa powder and/or confectioners' sugar.

Serve with one or more of the "kit" ideas on pages 24 and 26.

Nathalie's Melt-in-Your-Mouth Chocolate Cake

NO CORN SYRUP, NOT AN EGG IN SIGHT. All you need is some good chocolate. Now you've got no excuse for not decorating, glazing, or filling your desserts.

# Simple Dark Chocolate Glaze

**To cover a cake about 9 inches square
Preparation time: 2 minutes**

1 sheet of waxed paper
1 cake rack

7 ounces dark chocolate
½ cup unsalted butter
¼ cup water

Slowly melt all the ingredients in a microwave oven or in a bowl over hot water. Stir until the glaze is perfectly smooth.

Meanwhile, put the cake on the cake rack and then place it over the sheet of waxed paper, to catch the drips.

Allow the glaze to cool slightly, then spread over the cake.

# Extremely Easy Ganache

**To fill and top a cake about 9 inches in diameter
Preparation time: 5 minutes**

1 handheld electric mixer
1 spatula or broad-bladed knife

1½ cups whipping cream
12 ounces best-quality dark chocolate

Bring the cream to a boil and pour it over the chocolate. Allow the cream to melt the chocolate slightly, then stir until the mixture is smooth and glossy.

Place the ganache in a refrigerator for about 10 minutes. When cold, beat with the electric mixer until the mixture is light and airy.

Spread the ganache over the cake using a spatula.

# Traditional Butter Cream

**To fill and top a cake about 9 inches in diameter
Preparation time: 5 minutes**

1 handheld electric mixer
1 mixing bowl

1¼ cups confectioners' sugar
1 cup unsalted butter, preferably softened
2 tablespoons cocoa powder, dissolved in
3 tablespoons hot water

With the electric mixer, beat all the ingredients together in the bowl until the mixture is light and smooth.

# Very Rich Butter Cream

All the rest are just too light!

**To fill and top a cake about 9 inches in diameter
Preparation time: 5 minutes**

1 large mixing bowl

5 ounces best-quality dark chocolate
¼ cup unsalted butter
5 tablespoons milk
1 cup confectioners' sugar

Melt the chocolate and butter in the milk in a microwave oven or in a bowl over hot water.

Remove from the heat, incorporate the sugar, and mix well. Allow to cool before covering the cake.

# White or Milk Chocolate Butter Cream

**To fill and top a cake about 9 inches in diameter
Preparation time: 5 minutes**

1 handheld electric mixer

9 ounces white or milk chocolate
½ cup unsalted butter, softened
5 tablespoons mascarpone cheese
2 tablespoons confectioners' sugar

Melt the white or milk chocolate in a microwave oven or in a bowl over hot water.

Beat together the butter and mascarpone using the electric mixer. Add the melted chocolate, followed by the confectioners' sugar, beating until the mixture is light and airy.

## White, Milk, or Dark Chocolate Sauce

**Serves 6**
**Preparation time: 5 minutes**

1 saucepan

scant 1 cup whipping cream
½ cup milk
7 ounces white chocolate
or 5 ounces milk or semisweet chocolate

Bring the cream and milk almost to a boil, then pour them over the chocolate, stirring well. Serve hot or allow to cool.

## Chocolate Fudge Sauce

**Serves 6**
**Preparation time: 5 minutes**

1 saucepan

¼ cup unsalted butter
1½ cups whipping cream
1 cup soft brown sugar
6 ounces best-quality dark chocolate

Heat the butter, cream, and sugar until the sugar has totally dissolved. Add the chocolate and stir until melted. Allow to cool, then serve.

## Variations

### Chocolate-coffee

Dissolve 2 teaspoons of instant coffee in the cream mixture before adding the dark chocolate.

### Chocolate-orange

Add the grated rind of 1 orange to the sauce while still hot.

## Irish Coffee Sauce

**Serves 6**
**Preparation time: 5 minutes**

1 heavy saucepan

1 heaping cup sugar
2 teaspoons water
1 cup strong coffee
2 tablespoons Irish whiskey

Make a caramel with the sugar and water by heating in the saucepan over a low heat. Add the coffee, then allow to cool before adding the whiskey.

## Dark or White Chocolate Custard

**Serves 6–8**
**Preparation time: 5 minutes**
**Cooking time: 5 minutes**
**Cooling time: 2 hours**

1 saucepan
1 handheld electric mixer

2¼ cups milk
5 egg yolks
¼ cup sugar
2 ounces best-quality dark chocolate
or 4 ounces white chocolate
¼ cup sugar (optional)
1 vanilla bean (optional)

Heat the milk in the pan, but do not allow it to boil. Beat the egg yolks with the sugar until the mixture is pale and has doubled in volume. Pour the hot milk over the egg yolk mixture, stirring constantly. Return the creamy mixture to a fairly high heat, stirring constantly.

Cook until the mixture thickens sufficiently to coat the back of the spoon and your finger leaves a trace.

Melt the chocolate in the creamy mixture and stir.

Allow to cool for about 2 hours.

To make a traditional custard, add a vanilla bean to the milk and use an additional ¼ cup sugar.

## Caramel and Butter Sauce

**Serves 6**
**Cooking time: 5 minutes**

1 heavy saucepan

½ cup sugar
¼ cup unsalted butter
1½ cups whipping cream

To make the caramel, place the sugar in a thin layer over the base of the saucepan and melt. Remove from the heat and add the butter (don't worry if the mixture sets). Add the cream and reheat, stirring constantly.

## Variation

Add 1 teaspoon of cocoa powder or 1 teaspoon of instant coffee to vary the flavor.

WE CAN BE PUT OFF THE VERY IDEA OF CHOCOLATE MOUSSES. But, with good, fresh eggs, good-quality cream, and, of course, the very best chocolate, it's a dessert that everyone will love! All it takes to give it a new look is to play around with the quantities a little. Serve with little crisp cakes and cookies from a gourmet bakery.

# Extremely Easy Dark Chocolate Mousse

**Serves 4**
**Preparation time: 10 minutes**
**Chilling time: 2 hours**

1 handheld electric mixer

5 ounces semi- or bittersweet chocolate, chopped into small pieces
2 teaspoons rum, coffee liqueur, or brandy (optional)
5 eggs, separated

Melt the chocolate in a microwave oven or in a bowl over hot water. Remove from the heat and add the alcohol, if using. Then add the egg yolks, one by one.

Using the electric mixer, whisk the egg whites into stiff peaks and fold into the chocolate mixture. Pour the mixture into 1 large bowl or little individual ones.

Chill for at least 2 hours before serving.

# Slightly More Complicated Dark Chocolate Mousse

**Serves 6**
**Preparation time: 10 minutes**
**Chilling time: 2 hours**

1 handheld electric mixer

7 ounces best-quality dark chocolate, chopped into small pieces
¼ cup unsalted butter
3 eggs, separated
1½ cups heavy cream
3 tablespoons confectioners' sugar

Melt the chocolate with the butter in a microwave oven or in a bowl over hot water. In a separate bowl, combine the egg yolks with the cream, then add the confectioners' sugar. Add the melted chocolate and butter to the egg-cream mixture and stir well. In another bowl, using the electric mixer, whisk the egg whites into very stiff peaks and fold into the chocolate mixture.

Pour the mixture into a serving bowl or bowls.

Chill for at least 2 hours in the refrigerator.

# Milk Chocolate Mousse

**Serves 4**
**Preparation time: 5 minutes**
**Chilling time: overnight or 4 hours**

1 handheld electric mixer

½ cup whipping cream
5 ounces milk chocolate

Heat the cream and pour it over the chocolate. Stir well until the chocolate has melted and the mixture is smooth and glossy.

Chill overnight—or for at least 4 hours—in the refrigerator. Before serving, beat with the electric mixer and transfer to a serving bowl.

TIP • To decorate, make the Quick Caramel recipe on page 26, adding some roasted peanuts.

# White Chocolate Mousse

**Serves 6**

½ cup whipping cream
8 ounces white chocolate

Proceed as for the Milk Chocolate Mousse.

SUGGESTION • Decorate with seasonal berries.

PAVÉS ARE WONDERFUL DESSERTS, SO RICH AND INTENSE IN FLAVOR THAT A SMALL PORTION REALLY IS QUITE SUFFICIENT. They must be prepared in advance to allow the chocolate to release all its flavors. Mix and match with the easily prepared decorations from page 24 and/or decorate them using the suggestions on page 26. Thanks to the new flexible molds, you can make them in any shape you like. You can smile serenely throughout dinner, secure in the knowledge that your guests are in for a treat!

## Chocolate and Marrons Glacés Pavé

**Serves 8**
**Preparation time: 10 minutes**
**Chilling time: 5–6 hours**

1 handheld electric mixer
1 cake pan or loaf pan

1 can chestnut puree (about 1 pound)
10 tablespoons (1¼ sticks) unsalted butter, softened
3 to 4 tablespoons Baileys or 2 to 3 tablespoons rum, brandy, etc. (optional)
11 ounces best-quality dark chocolate
a few marrons glacés, for serving
some mascarpone cheese, for serving

Line the base of a round, shallow baking pan, or a loaf pan if you want to serve thin slices, with plastic wrap.

Combine the chestnut puree with the butter and alcohol (if using) until the mixture is smooth.

Melt the chocolate in a microwave oven or in a bowl over hot water. Combine the two mixtures, then pour into the baking pan of your choice. If using a loaf pan, make sure that the corners are filled. Leave to chill in a refrigerator for at least 5 to 6 hours, or overnight if possible. Serve with the marrons glacés, either whole or crumbled, and a little mascarpone to give a hint of acidity.

## Triple Chocolate Pavé

**Serves 10**
**Preparation time: 15 minutes**
**Chilling time: 5 hours**

1 loaf pan, 11 inches long (preferably nonstick)
1 saucepan

9 ounces best-quality dark chocolate
10 ounces milk chocolate
11 ounces white chocolate
2¼ cups whipping cream

Unless the loaf pan is nonstick, line it with plastic wrap.

You will have to make the layers separately: Place the three types of chocolate in three separate bowls. Bring a scant 1 cup of the cream almost to a boil and pour it over the dark chocolate, stirring well until the mixture is smooth. Pour the mixture into the loaf pan and place in a refrigerator to set.

Repeat this procedure with the milk chocolate, then pour the mixture over the first layer of dark chocolate.

Finish with the white chocolate, using the rest of the cream. Place the pan in a refrigerator for 5 hours, or in the freezer if you wish to serve this pavé frozen.

## Virginie's Chocolate Pavé

Just like Nathalie's cake, this recipe, which first appeared in *Cooking with friends*, was such a success that I just had to include it in this book. A great classic that always makes a big impression.

**Serves 6**
**Preparation time: 40 minutes**
**Chilling time: 5–6 hours**

1 10-inch loaf pan
1 handheld electric mixer

14 ounces baking chocolate
½ cup unsalted butter
4 egg yolks
⅔ cup confectioners' sugar
2¼ cups whipping cream, whipped

Melt the chocolate with the butter in a microwave oven or in a bowl over hot water.

Beat the egg yolks with the sugar until the mixture is pale.

Combine the two mixtures, beating with the electric mixer, then add the whipped cream. Transfer the mixture to a loaf pan lined with plastic wrap, or you can use shaped pans for an effect like that in the photo opposite. Allow to chill in the refrigerator for 5 to 6 hours.

I feel compelled to address the bizarre combinations of ingredients that have been so fashionable of late, such as pepper or Roquefort ganaches. It may be amusing to taste them at trendy restaurants, to tickle the taste buds, and educate the palate a little, but when you are cooking for family or friends, I find that it's best to avoid experimenting. The trick is to combine simplicity with good ingredients. Citrus fruits and berries add flavor and lightness to chocolate desserts, which can become almost sickly sweet.

# Citrus fruits

The bitterness of citrus fruits goes well with chocolate. Here are a few tricks that will turn your cakes, mousses, and tarts into the simplest of desserts worthy of the most stylish of dinners.

## Kumquats

You can find these in the produce section of major supermarkets. Very small, but very bitter, they are best if preserved in syrup, either whole or sliced, before serving. You can buy them preserved from gourmet food stores.

## Oranges

Orange is one of the flavors that goes best with chocolate—dark, milk, or white. Use the grated rind to give a slightly more unusual flavor to your chocolate dishes. You can remove the rind in strips with a zester or paring knife, blanch the strips by soaking them for 30 seconds in simmering water, and then candy them in melted sugar. You can also buy delicious whole candied fruits from major supermarkets and gourmet food stores.

## Lemons, limes, and grapefruits

They may not have met with such unanimous approval as oranges, but a lemon ganache made by a top chocolatier really is unforgettable.

# Candied Citrus Fruits

**Serves 6**
**Cooking time: 20 minutes**

1 saucepan

1¼ cups sugar
2¼ cups water
6 or 7 whole kumquats, or the rind of 2 lemons or 1 large orange, cut into strips

Place the water, kumquats or rind, and the sugar in a saucepan and heat gently until the sugar has dissolved. Boil gently for 20 minutes to produce a syrup, then allow to cool.

# Berries

Some berries seem to have been made for chocolate. Raspberries and blackberries spring immediately to mind, but try cranberries, blueberries, cherries, or boysenberries for a change. With the exception of cranberries, there's no need to cook them when they are in season.

Just serve a few with a cake, with a dollop of whipped cream, for example.

When made into a puree, they add a touch of moisture to a rather dry cake. Out of season, you can find a wide selection of frozen berries, which are superb cooked with just a little water and sugar. To make a smoother puree, pass the fruits through a strainer to remove the seeds and add some confectioners' sugar to make the mixture a bit sweeter.

Other acidic fruits, such as apricots, green apples, pineapple, mangoes, and passion fruit, also go very well with chocolate.

# Cranberries with Orange Rind

**Serves 6**
**Cooking time: 5 minutes**

1 saucepan

9 ounces fresh or frozen cranberries
2–3 tablespoons water
⅓ cup sugar
rind of 1 small orange

Place the cranberries in a saucepan with the water and sugar and cook for about 5 minutes. The cranberries will make some juice, but most of them will remain whole.

Add the rind, along with a little more sugar if it tastes too acidic, and allow to cool.

Serve with dark chocolate pavés or cakes.

# Quick Caramel

**Makes about 5 tablespoons of caramel**
**Cooking time: 3 minutes**

1 small, heavy saucepan
1 marble slab

**½ cup superfine sugar**

Cover the base of the pan with the sugar and heat gently. Stir with a wooden spoon until the sugar caramelizes and is completely transparent. Be careful not to overcook it, as this produces a bitter taste.

Pour straight onto a marble slab, quickly making it into the desired shape before it sets.

SUGGESTIONS • You can add hazelnuts, almonds, or even peanuts to add to the crunch. To make chocolate caramel, add 1 teaspoon cocoa powder. Adding cream and salted butter makes a deliciously smooth caramel sauce. Don't worry if the caramel "spits" a lot and sets. It will melt again if you stir it while heating the mixture gently.

TIP • To clean the pan, just fill it with hot water and heat it until all the sugar dissolves.

# Roasted Caramelized Almonds

**Makes 6**
**Preparation time: 3 minutes**

1 sheet of waxed paper
1 cookie sheet

**2 tablespoons corn syrup**
**1¼ cups slivered almonds**
**1 tablespoon confectioners' sugar**

Preheat the oven to 350°F.

Combine the syrup with the almonds.

Using a cookie cutter, steel ring, or simply the back of a spoon, arrange disks of the mixture on the waxed paper. Sprinkle with confectioners' sugar and bake for about 2 minutes until the almonds are golden.

Remove from the oven, reshape if necessary while the caramel is still soft, then allow to cool and set completely.

Store in an airtight container if you do not wish to serve them until the following day. They are best prepared just a few hours before the meal, as they tend to absorb any humidity in the room and become soft.

TIP • To make attractive irregular shapes, just spread a layer of caramelized almonds over the sheet, allow to cool and set, then break it into pieces.

Roasted Caramelized Almonds                    Chocolate t

THEY ALWAYS MAKE SUCH AN IMPRESSION, especially if you go to the trouble of making your own crust. These recipes are so easy that you won't buy a store-bought crust again. One small thing: Get yourself some metal pie weights to weigh down the crust when you bake it blind. They conduct the heat better than dried beans or rice and cook the crust more evenly. And what's more, you won't waste beans and rice, and you'll avoid the risk of giving your guests an unpleasant—and rather crunchy—surprise if you leave one behind in the base of the tart. The string shown in the photo (opposite) is wonderful, as you can pull out all the "beans" at once and never have to resort to using the tip of a knife, as might otherwise be the case.

## *Tart crust*
# Sweet Crust

**To make a tart shell about 10 inches in diameter**
**Preparation time: 5 minutes**
**Chilling time: 2 hours**

2 cups all-purpose flour
2 tablespoons sugar
½ cup very cold unsalted butter, cut into
small pieces
3–4 tablespoons very cold water

Place the flour and sugar in a large mixing bowl, add the butter, and rub in with your fingertips until the mixture resembles fine breadcrumbs. This can also be done in a food processor.

Make a well in the center and add the water. Combine with a wooden spoon, then knead by hand to form a ball of dough. Cover with plastic wrap and chill the pastry in the refrigerator for at least 2 hours before using.

# Chocolate Sweet Crust

**To make a tart shell about 11 inches in diameter**
**Preparation time: 5 minutes**
**Chilling time: 2 hours**

2 cups all-purpose flour
scant 1 cup confectioners' sugar
1 pinch of salt
1 tablespoon cocoa powder
14 tablespoons (1¾ sticks) very cold unsalted
butter, cut into pieces
2 egg yolks, lightly beaten with 1 tablespoon
water

Place all the dry ingredients in a large mixing bowl, add the butter, and rub in with your fingertips until the mixture resembles fine breadcrumbs. This can also be done in a food processor.

Make a well in the center and add the egg yolks and water. Combine using a wooden spoon, then knead by hand to form a ball of dough. Cover with plastic wrap and place in the refrigerator for at least 2 hours before using.

# Almond Sweet Crust

**To make a tart shell about 12 inches in diameter**
**or about 10 tartlets measuring 4 inches**
**Preparation time: 5 minutes**
**Chilling time: 1 hour**

1⅓ cups all-purpose flour
½ cup confectioners' sugar
1 pinch of salt
⅔ cup ground almonds
½ cup very cold unsalted butter, cut into
small pieces
1 egg yolk
2 tablespoons very cold water

Place the flour, confectioners' sugar, salt, and ground almonds in the mixing bowl. Add the butter and rub in with your fingertips until the mixture resembles fine breadcrumbs. Lightly beat the egg yolk with the measured water and pour into the mixing bowl. Combine with a wooden spoon, then knead by hand to form a ball of dough. Wrap the dough in plastic wrap before placing in the refrigerator to chill for at least 1 hour.

SUGGESTION • You can use ground hazelnuts instead of ground almonds.

## *Baking blind*

Roll out the pastry and line the baking pan. Fill with pie weights, navy beans, chickpeas, or rice and bake in a preheated oven at 350°F for 15–20 minutes. Allow to cool before filling.

Chocolate Sweet Pastry

*The fillings*

# White Chocolate

**To fill a tart shell about 10 inches in diameter**
**Preparation time: 15 minutes**
**Chilling time: 1 hour**

1 handheld electric mixer

1 gelatin leaf
1 tablespoon very hot water
5 ounces white chocolate
1 egg yolk
scant 1 cup whipping cream

In a bowl, soften the gelatin in some cold water, then dissolve it in the measured hot water.

Melt the chocolate in a microwave oven or in a bowl over hot water, then allow to cool slightly before adding the egg yolk and the gelatin.

Allow to cool completely. In another bowl, whip the cream, fold it into the chocolate mixture, and fill the pastry case. Place in the refrigerator for 1 hour to set.

# Dark Chocolate

**To fill a tart shell about 11 inches in diameter**
**Preparation time: 10 minutes**
**Chilling time: 1 hour**

1 saucepan

scant 1 cup whipping cream
11 ounces best-quality dark chocolate
3 egg yolks
3 tablespoons unsalted butter

Heat the cream, pour it over the chocolate, and stir well. Then incorporate the egg yolks and the butter. Pour the mixture into the crust and allow to chill in the refrigerator for 1 hour.

TIP • When the crust has cooled, using a fork, crush 2 cups raspberries with a little sugar and spread over the base of the crust before adding the chocolate cream.

# Chocolate Praline

**To fill a tart shell about 11 inches in diameter**
**Preparation time: 5 minutes**

1 saucepan

scant 1 cup whipping cream
2 ounces best-quality dark chocolate
9 ounces hazelnut-flavored chocolate or chocolate-hazelnut spread

Bring the cream almost to a boil and pour it over the chocolate and hazelnut chocolate. Stir well and spread over the base of the baked and cooled crust. Allow to cool.

# Milk Chocolate and Caramel

**To fill a tart shell about 11 inches in diameter**
**Preparation time: 10 minutes**

2 saucepans

¼ cup sugar
scant 1 cup whipping cream
9 ounces milk chocolate

Make a caramel by heating the sugar in a heavy saucepan. Bring the cream to a boil in a second saucepan, then pour it over the caramel. Pour the caramel cream over the chocolate and stir well.

Spread the mixture over the base of the baked tart shell.

Dark Chocolate and Berry Tart

# Chocolate nibbles

With coffee and after dinner or lunch, what I need is a very good, very dark, and very small piece of chocolate.

But steer clear of almonds, hazelnuts, and other nuts coated in a chocolate-flavored substance, which smear and crunch and then disappear in ten seconds; they're not what's called for.

These little mouthfuls to nibble with coffee are always a great success, and in my house often take the place of dessert, especially at lunchtime.

The little chocolate crisps are always a welcome nibble with your morning cup of coffee or as an afternoon snack.

# Orangettes

**Makes about 30**
**Preparation time: 30 minutes**

1 saucepan
1 sheet of waxed paper

4 ounces best-quality dark chocolate
3½ ounces strips of candied orange peel

Melt the chocolate in a microwave oven or in a bowl over hot water. Dip the strips of candied orange peel in the chocolate one at a time, coat each strip in chocolate, allowing any excess chocolate to drip back into the bowl, then place on the sheet of waxed paper. Allow to cool.

# Tuiles

**Makes about 20**
**Preparation time: 30 minutes**
**Cooling time: 30–60 minutes**

1 sheet of waxed paper
1 tuile shaper

7 ounces best-quality chocolate (dark, white, or milk)
1 tablespoon chopped, toasted hazelnuts or almonds, or slivered cocoa beans

Melt the chocolate in a microwave oven or in a bowl over hot water, then stir in the hazelnuts, almonds, or slivered cocoa beans. On the sheet of waxed paper, shape the mixture into very thin disks in sets of four. When the chocolate begins to set, use scissors to cut the waxed paper into strips and place them on the tuile shaper. Leave to set completely for 30–60 minutes, then turn the tuiles over and very carefully remove the strips of waxed paper.

# Rochers

**Makes about 20**
**Preparation time: 40 minutes**

1 cookie sheet
1 saucepan
1 sheet of waxed paper

4 ounces slivered almonds
2 tablespoons corn syrup
1 tablespoon confectioners' sugar
5 ounces best-quality dark or milk chocolate

Preheat the oven to 350°F. Combine the almonds with the corn syrup and shape into small mounds on a nonstick cookie sheet. Sprinkle with the confectioners' sugar, then bake for 2–3 minutes, until the sugar caramelizes. Leave to cool. Melt the chocolate in a microwave oven or in a bowl over hot water, dip the rochers in the chocolate one at a time, and then place them on the sheet of waxed paper.

TIP • If you can't find any slivered almonds at the store, make your own by cutting whole almonds lengthwise.

# Truffles

**Makes 30–40 truffles**
**Preparation time: 5 minutes**
**Chilling time: 2 hours**

1 saucepan

## The ganache

1 cup whipping cream
1 pound best-quality chocolate

## The decoration

dark or white chocolate, in drops, grated, or chopped into small pieces
cocoa powder
slivered cocoa beans
ground toasted hazelnuts or almonds

Bring the cream almost to a boil and pour it over the chocolate. Stir gently and leave to cool.

Using your fingers, shape the mixture into small balls and coat them in dark chocolate, white chocolate, cocoa powder, slivered cocoa beans, or ground toasted hazelnuts or almonds, then chill for about 2 hours.

## Mendiants

**Makes about 25**
**Preparation time: 30 minutes**

1 sheet of waxed paper

4 ounces best-quality dark chocolate
¼ cup raisins
1 tablespoon pistachio nuts
¼ cup blanched almonds
2 ounces candied orange peel

Place a sheet of waxed paper on a marble slab or other cold, smooth surface. Melt the chocolate in a microwave oven or in a bowl over hot water. Place a teaspoonful of melted chocolate on the sheet and spread it out with the back of the spoon to form a disk. Make several at a time so that the chocolate does not cool before you have finished. Place a raisin, pistachio nut, almond, and a small strip of candied orange peel on each disk and leave to cool completely.

The mendiants are ready when they lift off the paper easily.

## Ganache Prunes

Chocolate and prunes are a magic mixture that draws out the aroma of the fruit. This is a little delicacy to serve as a lunchtime dessert, or with an after-dinner coffee even if a dessert has already been served.

**Serves 6**
**Preparation time: 5 minutes**
**Cooling time: 10 minutes**

1 saucepan
1 handheld electric mixer
1 pastry bag

½ cup whipping cream
4 ounces dark chocolate, chopped into small pieces
12 or 18 prunes, pitted

Bring the cream almost to a boil and pour it over the chocolate. Leave the cream to melt the chocolate a little, then stir until the mixture is smooth and glossy. Using the handheld mixer, beat until the mixture attains a mousse-like consistency and has cooled.

Slit the prunes open to form butterfly shapes. Fill the pastry bag with the ganache mixture and pipe a generous dollop inside each prune, then gently press each prune shut.

SUGGESTION • Coat the prunes in 11 ounces melted dark chocolate. You could also add 1 or 2 tablespoons of Armagnac to the ganache mixture.

## Chocolate-Coated Fruits

**Makes 14 ounces**
**Preparation time: 5 minutes**
**Cooling time: 1 hour**

1 sheet of waxed paper
1 dipping fork or 2 forks

9 ounces best-quality chocolate
7 ounces dried fruits (apricots, prunes, dates, figs, pears, etc.)

Melt the chocolate in a microwave oven or in a bowl over hot water. Drop the fruits in the melted chocolate one by one, coat completely, then remove them using two forks or, better still, a chocolate-maker's dipping fork, allowing any excess chocolate to drip back into the bowl. Place them on the waxed paper and leave them at room temperature for 30–60 minutes to set.

## Chocolate Disks

**Makes 14 ounces**
**Preparation time: 10 minutes**
**Cooling time: 1 hour**

1 sheet of waxed paper

9 ounces best-quality chocolate
2 cups hazelnuts or almonds

Melt the chocolate in a microwave oven or in a bowl over hot water. Add the nuts and stir gently. Arrange small mounds of the chocolate mixture on the waxed paper. Press down slightly with the back of a spoon to make small circles. Leave to set at room temperature for 30–60 minutes.

Chocolate nibbles          Easter Eggs

# Easter Eggs

Here's a wholesome and easy activity for the children at Easter time. All you will really have to do is find an egg-shaped mold.

**Makes 4 halves, each about 4 inches long**
**Preparation time: 25 minutes**
**Cooling time: 40 minutes**

1 saucepan
1 egg-shaped mold

**1 pound best-quality dark or milk chocolate**
**1 box of breakfast cereal**

Melt the chocolate in a microwave oven or in a bowl over hot water.

Combine the melted chocolate with the cereal until it is thoroughly coated.

Now you have a choice: You can fill the molds completely to make solid egg halves, or you can coat the surface of the molds with a layer of the mixture to make hollow egg halves. The first option is definitely the easiest for children; the second requires a little dexterity. You need to start at the center of the mold, gradually adding more mixture to "construct" the sides. Be careful not to press the mixture down too hard against the sides of the mold so that the egg does not lose its appealingly rustic, homemade look.

Leave the eggs to cool and set in a refrigerator for about 40 minutes. Twist the mold as you would an ice-cube tray to release the egg halves and turn them out.

Decorate with ribbons. The children can wrap their masterpieces in decorative paper, make pretty labels, and give them as presents.

# Small Molded Shapes

In this recipe more than all the rest, the quality of the chocolate is the key to success. Couverture chocolate, so rich in cocoa butter, is perfect for all molded shapes, whether large or small.

**Makes 50 small shapes**
**Preparation time: 10 minutes**
**Cooling time: 30–60 minutes**

1 small chocolate shapes mold
1 sheet of waxed paper
1 angled spatula (see page 150)

**11 ounces best-quality chocolate**

Melt the chocolate in a microwave oven or in a bowl over hot water.

Pour the melted chocolate into the mold, making sure that each shape is filled and that all the chocolate is spread out by tapping the base of the mold for a few seconds to release any air bubbles that could spoil the surface of the chocolate shapes.

Scrape any excess chocolate off the mold onto the sheet of waxed paper or into a large bowl. Be careful not to leave any chocolate between the shapes, as this will make them more difficult to turn out from the mold and will make the shapes less well defined.

Leave the mold to cool at room temperature for a few minutes, then transfer to a refrigerator for 30–60 minutes.

The shapes will be ready to turn out when the chocolate has come away from the edges. To turn the chocolates out, twist the mold slightly as you would an ice-cube tray. When the chocolate lifts, making a snap, you can carefully turn the mold over and remove the shapes. If you don't hear a snap, refrigerate for another 20 minutes.

TIP • If you have tempered the chocolate, the shapes will stay glossy; if not, they may tarnish after 24 hours, but even so they will without doubt still be edible! Use the remaining chocolate to make candies, for example, or it can even be used to make a cake, mousse, or cup of hot chocolate.

# Florentines (well, almost!)

There are some recipes that always elude us! I have tried to make real Florentines, tested three different recipes, and used up quantities of candied cherries and fruits. But I have never managed it, and I don't know why! So here's my own recipe, which contains most of the ingredients (except the stress) of the real thing.

**Makes about 12**
**Preparation time: 20 minutes**
**Cooking time: 25 minutes**

1 cookie sheet
1 saucepan
2 sheets of waxed paper

½ cup unsalted butter
⅔ cup soft brown sugar
4 tablespoons honey
½ cup candied cherries
½ cup raisins
⅓ cup candied fruits, chopped
1 cup slivered almonds
scant 1 cup all-purpose flour
4 ounces best-quality dark or milk chocolate

Preheat the oven to 350°F.

Grease a jelly-roll pan measuring roughly 11 x 7 inches and line the base with waxed paper.

Heat the butter, sugar, and honey until the sugar has dissolved completely. Remove from the heat and add the cherries, raisins, candied fruits, almonds, and flour. Stir well. Transfer to the jelly-roll pan and bake for 20–25 minutes or until golden on top.

Leave to cool in the pan for 5 minutes, then mark into squares with a knife; they will be easier to cut when they have cooled.

When cooled, melt the chocolate in a microwave oven or in a bowl over hot water. Separate the Florentines with your fingers and dip one side into the chocolate, then place on a sheet of waxed paper and leave to cool once more.

# Biscotti

**Makes about 30**
**Preparation time: 20 minutes**
**Chilling time: 30 minutes**
**Cooking time: 35 minutes**

1 handheld electric mixer
cookie sheets
waxed paper

1 heaping cup sugar
6 tablespoons unsalted butter, softened
4 eggs
1 teaspoon vanilla extract
1¾ cups all-purpose flour
1 tablespoon baking powder
9 ounces best-quality dark chocolate chips

Preheat the oven to 350°F.

Beat the sugar and butter. Add the eggs one by one, then the vanilla. Incorporate the flour and baking powder. Add the chocolate chips and mix well. On waxed paper, shape the mixture into two rectangles, 10 inches long and 4 inches wide. Refrigerate for 30 minutes.

Place on a cookie sheet and bake for 25 minutes. The cake should be crackled on top and a knife inserted into the center should come out clean. Remove from the oven and cool for 10 minutes. Reduce the oven temperature to 300°F.

Slip the cakes onto a board and, while still hot, cut diagonally into ½-inch-thick slices. Place the biscotti, on their sides, on cookie sheets and bake again for 5–8 minutes each side. They should be golden on top. Leave to cool, then indulge yourself by dunking them in a cup of good coffee.

# Pistachio and Ginger Shortbread

**Serves 6–8**
**Makes about 15**
**Preparation time: 15 minutes**
**Total cooking time: 50 minutes**

1 cookie sheet
1 sheet of waxed paper

⅓ cup sugar
2⅔ cups all-purpose flour
½ cup plus 2 tablespoons very cold butter, cut into small pieces
½ cup pistachio nuts
3 tablespoons preserved ginger, cut into small pieces
5 ounces best-quality dark, white, or milk chocolate

Preheat the oven to 350°F.

Place the sugar and flour in a bowl, add the butter, and rub in with your fingertips until it resembles fine breadcrumbs. This can also be done in a food processor. Add the pistachio nuts and ginger. Knead for one minute on a cold, lightly floured surface.

Roll the mixture out on a cold surface and cut into shapes of your choice.

Place on a cookie sheet and bake for 25–30 minutes.

Remove from the oven, sprinkle with sugar, allow to cool for a few minutes, then transfer to a wire rack.

Melt the chocolate. Dip the shortbread cookies in the melted chocolate. Leave to cool once more on a sheet of waxed paper.

# Chocolate Shortbread

**Serves 6–8**
**Makes about 20 pieces**
**Preparation time: 15 minutes**
**Cooking time: 50 minutes**

1 fluted, round, shallow baking pan

2½ cups all-purpose flour
⅓ cup sugar
3½ tablespoons cocoa powder
½ cup plus 2 tablespoons very cold butter, cut into small pieces
confectioners' sugar, for dusting

Preheat the oven to 300°F.

Place the flour, sugar, and cocoa powder in a bowl, add the butter, and rub in with your fingertips until the mixture resembles fine breadcrumbs. This can also be done in a food processor. Knead for one minute on a cold, lightly floured surface. Press the mixture into the greased baking pan with your fingers.

Bake for 50 minutes.

Remove from the oven, cut into triangles, and sprinkle with confectioners' sugar. Leave to cool in the pan.

Pistachio and Ginger Shortbread

# Double Chocolate Peanut Butter Cookies

With two types of chocolate chips, plus cocoa powder, this recipe doesn't skimp on that great chocolate taste. The savory flavor of the peanuts creates a wonderful contrast. These very rich cookies really are better if made very small.

**Makes about 36 cookies**
**Preparation time: 15 minutes**
**Cooking time: 15 minutes**

2 cookie sheets
waxed paper

**The cookies**
4 ounces best-quality dark chocolate
½ cup butter
1½ cups sugar
3 eggs, beaten
scant 1 cup all-purpose flour
1½ teaspoons baking powder
1 cup cocoa powder
4 ounces milk chocolate, cut into about
½-inch pieces

**The filling**
⅔ cup peanut butter
6 tablespoons confectioners' sugar

Preheat the oven to 325°F.

Melt the dark chocolate with the butter in a microwave oven or in a bowl over hot water. Leave to cool, then add the sugar, followed by the eggs. Add the flour, baking powder, and cocoa powder. Stir well, then incorporate the milk chocolate pieces.

Take a teaspoonful of the mixture and rub it between the palms of your hands to form a small ball, then place on the cookie sheet and press down lightly.

Repeat for the rest of the mixture, leaving about 2 inches between the cookies, then bake for 12–15 minutes. Remove from the oven and transfer to a wire rack to cool.

Mix together the peanut butter and confectioners' sugar. Spread on one cookie, then top with a second cookie, lightly pressing them together so they do not fall apart.

Serve with coffee or as a dessert with some vanilla ice cream.

# Classic chocolate
## (but not over the top)

If you ever get the chance to visit the kitchen of a great pastry chef, you will immediately appreciate that there is a real difference between what we humble amateur cooks can achieve and what those wonderful magicians manage to create every day . . .

The professionals have the equipment, but above all they have a talent and knowledge that I never even suspected until I had seen them at work. It is always fascinating to watch them, and we can take home with us some of their tricks and techniques that are within our reach.

But frankly, I'm convinced that what matters most is to make sure we use top-quality ingredients and have confidence in our own methods, and leave the overly elaborate, the complex, and the sophisticated to the professional confectioner!

A real homemade cake made with the best chocolate will give your guests just as much pleasure (and you a great deal less anxiety) than a rather unsuccessful attempt at copying the professionals!

The "classic" recipes included in this chapter have thus been adapted slightly. While I may have simplified or played around with them a bit, I have always retained the basic flavors and associations.

Chocolate-iced cream puff made by Ladurée

# Chocolate Tiramisu

A great classic, bordering on the commonplace as a result of all the pale industrial imitations that have overrun our supermarket shelves. So, to give a bit of moral support to tiramisu, here's a recipe that's more than classic—with a little dark chocolate, simply to justify including this recipe in this book.

**Serves 6**
**Preparation time: 30 minutes**
**Chilling time: 5 hours**

1 serving dish or 6 individual bowls
1 handheld electric mixer

6 eggs, separated
½ cup sugar
1 pound mascarpone cheese
1 glass of amaretto liqueur or marsala
1 cup warm, strong coffee
30 ladyfingers
7 ounces best-quality dark chocolate
¼ cup cocoa powder

Beat the egg yolks with the sugar until the mixture is pale. Incorporate the mascarpone and continue to beat. Whisk three egg whites into stiff peaks and fold into the mascarpone, egg, and sugar mixture.

Add the amaretto to the coffee. Briefly soak the ladyfingers in this mixture and arrange them in the bottom of the dish(es). Melt the chocolate in a microwave oven or in a bowl over hot water. Cover the ladyfingers with the creamy mixture, then top with a thin layer of melted chocolate.

Repeat this procedure to create the second layer.

Cover with plastic wrap and leave to chill for at least 5 hours in the refrigerator.

Sprinkle with cocoa powder just before serving.

# Banoffee

In the United States and Britain, banoffee has become so popular that it is almost replacing mom's apple pie. The reason for this extraordinary success? The unique flavor combination of its ingredients: bananas with caramel on a cookie-crumb base with a pinch of salt. All it needs is the chocolate.

**Serves 6**
**Preparation time: 2 hours for the caramel, 20 minutes for the rest**
**Chilling time: 2 hours**

6 stainless steel circles, 3 inches in diameter
1 saucepan
1 handheld electric mixer

**14-ounce can sweetened condensed milk**
**½ cup graham cracker crumbs**
**1 tablespoon unsalted butter**
**3 bananas, sliced**
**juice of 1 lemon**
**7 ounces milk chocolate**
**whipping cream, to serve**

Make a small hole in the can of condensed milk, place it in a pan of simmering water, and leave to simmer over low heat for 2 hours. Remove the can from the pan and leave to cool.

Melt the butter and combine with the graham cracker crumbs. Place a stainless steel ring on each plate, then press the mixture into the base of each ring. Leave to cool.

Toss the sliced bananas in the lemon juice to keep them from turning brown, then arrange them on the crumb bases. Pour the caramelized milk over the bananas.

Melt the chocolate in a microwave oven or in a bowl over hot water. Pour the chocolate over the caramel and leave to chill and set in a refrigerator for 1–2 hours.

Just before serving, whip the cream, then carefully remove the rings by gently pressing down on the chocolate disks. Decorate with a little whipped cream and leave the banoffee to settle and ooze out deliciously on each plate.

## Honey and Chocolate Madeleines

**Makes about 40 small or 20 large cakes**
**Preparation time: 10 minutes**
**Chilling time: 1 hour**
**Cooking time: 8–10 minutes per tray**

1 muffin pan (shell-shaped cups, nonstick if possible)

5 ounces best-quality dark chocolate
5 tablespoons unsalted butter
5 eggs, separated
¼ cup honey
½ cup sugar
1⅓ cups all-purpose flour

Preheat the oven to 375°F.

Melt the chocolate and butter in a microwave oven or in a bowl over hot water and allow to cool.

Beat the egg yolks with the sugar until the mixture is thick and pale. Add the melted chocolate, honey, sugar, and flour, beating the mixture at high speed after each addition.

Whisk the egg whites into soft peaks and fold into the mixture.

Leave the mixture to chill in a refrigerator for at least 1 hour.

If you are using a nonstick pan, there is no need to grease it; if you are using a traditional, shell-shaped pan, grease the cups thoroughly.

Use a level teaspoonful of the mixture for small cakes, a heaping teaspoonful for large cakes.

Bake for 8–10 minutes, depending on the size of the cakes. They should have risen slightly on top. Remove from the oven and leave to cool slightly before turning them out.

## Poires Belle-Hélène

The classic version calls for vanilla ice cream, poached pears, and a rich, hot chocolate sauce (purists among you can use the Chocolate Sauce recipe on page 18). The following recipe is easy to make; some flavors have been added to make it unique. The combination of pear, caramel, chocolate, and coffee is excellent, as is the contrast in temperatures. I use an ice cream containing little pieces of caramel for a touch of crispness.

**Serves 6**
**Preparation time: 15 minutes**

6 ice-cream glasses
2 saucepans

12 large, fresh pears or 12 canned pears
½ quart caramel ice cream
1 portion Chocolate-Coffee Sauce (see page 18)

Peel and core the fresh pears and divide into quarters.

Place a few portions in each glass, add the ice cream, and pour the hot sauce on top. Serve immediately.

Honey and Chocolate Madeleines

Honey and Chocolate Madeleines

# Mango, Pineapple, and Ginger Upside-Down Dessert

A variation of the dessert that has nothing in common with the version that I remember from my school's cafeteria.

**Serves 8**
**Preparation time: 15 minutes**
**Cooking time: 45 minutes**

1 handheld electric mixer
1 square cake pan or 1 gratin dish
1 sheet of aluminum foil

1 fresh mango
¼ fresh pineapple
9 ounces best-quality dark chocolate, chopped or in chips
½ cup unsalted butter
⅓ cup sugar
2 eggs
⅔ cup all-purpose flour
1 teaspoon baking powder
1 tablespoon preserved ginger, chopped into small pieces (if you cannot find any, use 2–3 teaspoons ground ginger according to taste)

Grease a gratin dish or 9-inch-square cake pan.

Preheat the oven to 350°F.

Peel the mango and pineapple and cut into 1-inch cubes.

Melt 6 ounces chocolate and all the butter in a microwave oven or in a bowl over hot water.

Beat the sugar with the eggs, then add the melted chocolate and butter. Fold in the flour, baking powder, ginger, and the remaining chocolate pieces. Place the fruit in the dish and spread the chocolate mixture on top.

Bake for 45 minutes, covering with foil after 30 minutes.

Turn out and serve, fruit-side up.

Classic chocolate

# Black Forest Trifle

The same principle as the famous cake, but in a different form and with a bit more chocolate.

**Serves 12**
**Preparation time: 30 minutes**
**Cooking time: 20 minutes**
**Chilling time: 2 hours**

2 shallow baking pans, about 9 inches in diameter
1 handheld electric mixer
1 large glass serving bowl
1 sheet of waxed paper

12 eggs, separated
1 cup sugar
¾ cup cocoa powder
1 large jar (or 2 small jars) Morello cherries, with cherry liqueur if possible
2¼ cups whipping cream
8 ounces mascarpone cheese (optional)
3 tablespoons sugar
7 ounces best-quality dark chocolate
4 ounces dark chocolate, shaved

Preheat the oven to 350°F.

Grease the baking pans and line with waxed paper.

Beat the egg yolks with the sugar until the mixture is pale and frothy. Fold in the cocoa powder using a large spoon. Beat the egg whites into peaks and fold into the chocolate mixture in three batches to keep the egg whites from collapsing.

Pour into the baking pans and bake for about 20 minutes. The top of the cake should be soft to the touch. Remove from the oven and leave to cool slightly on a wire rack, then turn out and leave to cool completely.

Drain the cherries, reserving the syrup.

Beat the cream with the sugar and mascarpone (if using).

Cut both cakes in half horizontally to create four layers and place one layer in the bottom of the serving dish. Pour half the cherry syrup on top and arrange the fruits over the sponge cake.

Melt the chocolate in a microwave oven or in a bowl over hot water. Spoon the chocolate over the cherries and cake layer as thinly as possible, so that it sets when it comes into contact with the cake. Place a layer of the cream mixture over the chocolate, then repeat the procedure for the next layers, reserving a few cherries and the shaved chocolate for the final decoration.

Leave to chill in the refrigerator for a few hours before serving.

# Sacher Torte (or nearly)

The prince of chocolate cakes! Real Sacher torte has a thin layer of apricot puree, concealed beneath a perfectly smooth dark chocolate glaze bearing the word "Sacher" written in milk chocolate. Unfortunately, the latter two stages are beyond me. I have always found that the apricots are in rather short supply in relation to the copious and extremely rich sponge cake. Purists will scream, perhaps, there will be a flood of criticism, and Herr Sacher will turn in his grave, but this adjusted version, with its different combination of flavors, works well.

**Serves 6**
**Preparation time: 20 minutes**
**Cooking time: 30 minutes**
**Cooling time: 1 hour**

6 stainless steel rings about 2½ inches in diameter, or
1 muffin pan (preferably flexible)
1 cookie sheet, to hold the rings
1 saucepan

4 ounces best-quality dark chocolate
5 tablespoons unsalted butter, softened
¼ cup sugar
4 eggs, separated
½ cup all-purpose flour

## For the apricot sauce

3 tablespoons apricot jelly
juice of 1 lemon
about 10 dried apricots, finely diced

## For the glaze

4 ounces best-quality dark chocolate
¼ cup unsalted butter
2 tablespoons water

Preheat the oven to 350°F.

Melt the chocolate in a microwave oven or in a bowl over hot water.

Cream the butter with the sugar until the mixture is light and fluffy. Add the egg yolks one by one, beating after each addition. Add the melted chocolate, stir well, and incorporate the flour.

Beat the egg whites into stiff peaks and fold into the chocolate mixture (in three batches, so they do not collapse).

Transfer the mixture to the baking rings or muffin pan and bake for 20–25 minutes until the cakes are well risen; a skewer inserted into the center of each cake should come out clean. Remove from the oven and leave to cool slightly in the rings or pan on a wire rack, then turn out and cool completely.

Heat the jelly with the lemon juice, diced apricot, and a little water. Poach for about 5 minutes until the apricots are soft. Leave to cool. If the sauce is too thick, add a little water.

To make the glaze, melt the chocolate and butter with the water in a microwave oven or in a bowl over hot water.

Cut the cakes in half horizontally and place one half on each individual plate. Pour a tablespoon of apricot sauce over each, top with the remaining cake halves, then spoon a little glaze on top. You can either serve the cakes immediately or wait until the glaze has set.

# Chocotherapy

# Chocotherapy

Chocolate is really good for solving problems. A bout of the blues, a stressful day, an argument, a reward, a secret pleasure? Chocolate always has the answer.

You don't need the same chocolate for every occasion. In my moments of anxiety, the only thing that will do is a whole bar of chocolate wolfed down in thirty seconds. But, it's sweet, it has hardly any flavor, it sticks to your palate, I hear you cry? So much the better! Those are exactly the sensations I'm looking for. A substitute for the mother's breast, Freud would say. I don't know and I don't care—it works.

If I'm having a cup of coffee with girlfriends, talking about men/children/clothes/television, then the good old triple chocolate cake with frosting and/or custard is just the thing to give us a good helping of collective guilt and make us feel obliged to moan about our various rolls of fat and cellulose—and even compare them: "Do you really think my calves have slimmed down? Oh, go on, just a little taste, then."

Some recipes, like rice pudding or chocolate cream, take us back to our childhoods and wrap us in a great cocoon of chocolate, which does us good; other recipes combine the voluptuousness of the chocolate with the kick of the alcohol. Everyone has their own cure. In this chapter you are sure to find the one that suits you!

Ireland, where I come from, has always had recipes for "cannibal" cakes: making a different cake from one that's already cooked! It's not that my mother and her friends were particularly avant-garde or that they sensed trends twenty years in advance, but rather for reasons of speed and ease. "Creative combinations" such as the Sausage, Marshmallow Squares, and the Nanaimo Bar have thus proved a success at countless midmorning coffee get-togethers in Ireland. The recipes are fabulously rich and should therefore be enjoyed with more restraint than some of the other recipes in this book.

# Chocolate French Toast

**Serves 8**
**Preparation time: 15 minutes**
**Resting time: at least 12 hours (overnight)**
**Cooking time: 30 minutes**

1 gratin dish

About 10 slices of stale bread, crusts removed
5 ounces best-quality dark chocolate
5 tablespoons unsalted butter
½ cup sugar
2¼ cups whipping cream
4 eggs
A little sour cream, if you like, and dark brown
sugar to serve

Lightly grease the gratin dish.

Cut the bread into triangles.

Melt the chocolate and butter with the sugar and
cream in a microwave oven or in a bowl over hot
water. Stir well and make sure the sugar is well
dissolved. Lightly beat the eggs, add them to the
mixture, then beat again until the mixture is
smooth and creamy.

Place the bread in the gratin dish so the slices
overlap. Pour the chocolate sauce on top, pressing
down with a spoon to ensure that the slices are
well covered. Leave to soak for at least a whole
day if possible.

Preheat the oven to 350°F. Bake for about
30 minutes. Leave to cool slightly before serving
with a little sour cream and dark brown sugar.

SUGGESTION • You can make this recipe even
richer by using brioche or panettone instead of
ordinary bread.

# Rice Pudding with a Melted Chocolate Heart

This is not so much a recipe as it is a delicious
trick that is sure to delight your guests and raise
your spirits as you wallow in a great wave of
comforting nostalgia.

**Serves 6**
**Preparation time: 5 minutes**
**Cooking time: 20 minutes**

1 saucepan
6 ramekins

3½ cups milk
½ cup sugar
1 vanilla bean
2½ cups short-grain rice
5 ounces best-quality dark chocolate, chopped
into ½-inch pieces, or chocolate chips

Bring the milk and sugar almost to a boil in a
saucepan. Split the vanilla bean lengthwise and
add to the milk mixture along with the rice.
Cook for about 20 minutes, stirring constantly,
until the milk has been absorbed and the rice is
soft, adding more milk if the mixture is too sticky.

Spoon the rice mixture into the ramekin dishes.
Using a small spoon, press the chocolate pieces
into the rice, spooning the rice back on top to
conceal the chocolate. By the time your guests
plunge in their spoons, the chocolate will have
melted, presenting them with a serious dilemma:
to stir or not to stir?

SUGGESTION • Alternatively, you can use dark
or milk chocolate, and stir it in immediately.
Place a spoonful of mascarpone cheese or sour
cream on top, with a sprinkling of brown sugar
for a crunchy touch. It's just too good for words!

Rice Pudding with a Melted Chocolate Heart

## Basque Yogurt with Homemade Chocolate Sauce

**Preparation time: 5 minutes**

1 large screw-top jar

7 ounces dark couverture chocolate
1¼ cups plus 2 tablespoons margarine
14-ounce can sweetened condensed milk
¾ cup ground almonds or hazelnuts

Melt the chocolate in a microwave oven or in a bowl over hot water. Add the margarine, followed by the milk and ground nuts, and stir well. Pour into a large screw-top jar and store in a cool place. Serve with yogurt.

## Petits Suisses with Chocolate Sauce

**Serves 3**
**Preparation time: 5 minutes**

1 saucepan

⅓ cup milk
⅔ cup light cream
5 ounces milk chocolate, finely chopped
6 small cylinders of Petits Suisses or any other very soft, smooth cream cheese

Heat the milk and cream, then pour the mixture over the chocolate. Stir and serve while still hot with the Petits Suisses.

You could, of course, just melt your favorite chocolate bars instead of making your own sauce!

Petits Suisses with Chocolate Sauce

# Little Chocolate Creams Like My Mother Used to Make

**Serves 6**
**Preparation time: 10 minutes**
**Cooking time: 20 minutes**

1 handheld electric mixer
1 gratin dish or baking pan
1 saucepan
6 small bowls or ramekins

5 eggs
⅓ cup sugar
2 cups milk
4 ounces best-quality dark chocolate, chopped into small pieces

Preheat the oven to 350°F.

Place the eggs and sugar in the mixing bowl and beat lightly. Bring the milk almost to a boil, pour it over the chocolate, and mix well.

Gradually add the chocolate mixture to the eggs.

Pour the creamy mixture into the little bowls or ramekins. Place them in a gratin dish or baking pan and fill it with hot water to the halfway mark.

Place in the oven and cook for 15–20 minutes. Leave to cool and serve with thin, crisp cookies.

# Chocolate Crème Brûlée

**Serves 6**
**Preparation time: 15 minutes**
**Cooking time: 30 minutes**
**Chilling time: 2 hours**

1 handheld electric mixer
6 individual gratin dishes or ramekins

5 ounces best-quality dark chocolate
7 egg yolks
¼ cup sugar
2½ cups whipping cream
5 tablespoons brown sugar

Preheat the oven to 250°F.

Melt the chocolate in a microwave oven or in a bowl over hot water, then leave to cool slightly.

Beat the egg yolks with the sugar using the electric mixer until the mixture is pale. Add the melted chocolate, then the cream, beating constantly.

Pour the mixture into the individual gratin dishes or ramekins and bake for about 30 minutes. Keep a close eye on them—the creamy mixture should be firm at the edges but not yet set in the middle.

Remove the ramekins from the oven and leave to cool before placing them in a refrigerator for several hours.

Just before serving, set the oven to broil, sprinkle the cream-filled ramekins with brown sugar, caramelize them under the broiler, and then return them to a cool place.

# Floating Islands in a Chocolate Lake

**Serves 6**
**Preparation time: 20 minutes**
**Cooking time: 15 minutes**

1 saucepan
1 handheld electric mixer

**Chocolate custard**
2¼ cups milk
5 egg yolks
¼ cup sugar
2¼ ounces best-quality dark chocolate

**Islands**
5 egg whites
2½ tablespoons sugar
A little dark brown sugar and ½ cup toasted
hazelnuts or almonds to decorate

To make the chocolate custard, heat the milk but
do not allow to boil.

Using an electric mixer, beat the egg yolks with
the sugar until the mixture is pale and has
doubled in volume.

When the milk is almost at the boiling point,
pour it over the egg yolks, stirring constantly.
Return this mixture to a fairly high heat, stirring
constantly. Cook until the mixture coats the back
of the spoon.

Melt the chocolate in the creamy mixture, then
leave to cool completely before placing in a
refrigerator.

For the islands, whisk the egg whites into stiff
peaks. Add the sugar and whisk again.

Poach spoonfuls of the whisked egg white
mixture in a pan of simmering water for about
1 minute. Drain and leave to cool.

To serve, pour the chocolate cream into a small
dish and top with an island. Sprinkle with the
brown sugar and toasted or caramelized
hazelnuts or almonds.

SUGGESTION • You can also cook the egg whites
in a microwave oven. Place the islands one at a
time on the oven plate. Cook for five seconds on
high until the island expands.

# Hot Chocolate

Hot chocolate, like tea or coffee, is sacred. Each
has its own ritual. On the other hand, when
you have your friends over for a snack, or the
children's friends in the afternoon (as I am doing
more and more), hot chocolate—the real thing,
that is—is an extra-special treat.

**Serves 2**
**Preparation time: 2 minutes**

1 saucepan
1 hand whisk

**2½ ounces best-quality dark chocolate, in pieces**
**2 teaspoons sugar**
**1 vanilla bean, split**
**1 cup milk**
**½ cup cream**
**Cocoa powder or shaved chocolate**

Place all the ingredients in the saucepan and heat
gently, stirring with a hand whisk until all the
chocolate has melted and the mixture is hot and
frothy. Pour into cups and sprinkle with the cocoa
powder or shaved chocolate.

SUGGESTION • You could also whip up
some cream and place a spoonful on the
hot chocolate before serving.

Chocolate Granola

# Chocolate Granola

Just the ticket if you're suffering from an attack of the blues, when all you want to do is slump in front of the television and switch off mentally. Make it in large quantities, and you will never want to buy cereal from the store again. Adapt this recipe using your favorite grains; increase the quantities and omit ingredients to suit your own particular tastes.

**Preparation time: 5 minutes**
**Cooking time: 5 minutes**

1 baking tray

4 ounces dark chocolate chips
½ cup rolled oats
1 tablespoon pistachio nuts
1 tablespoon flaked almonds
1 tablespoon pecans (or whole hazelnuts, almonds, or macadamia nuts)
1 tablespoon grated coconut
1 tablespoon pine nuts
1 tablespoon honey

Preheat the oven to 350°F.

Mix the ingredients together thoroughly. Place on a baking tray and bake for 5–7 minutes or until the mixture turns beautifully golden. Shake the tray halfway through to keep the grains from sticking to each other. Leave to cool. Serve in a bowl with milk or yogurt and fresh fruit—while you sit there snug in your slippers.

SUGGESTION • See page 122 for a more elaborate recipe using this granola.

# Toasted Sandwiches

Forget the modern grilling, toasting, and waffle-making appliances. First you've got to plug them in, then clear them away, and anyone in need of a bit of instant chocotherapy knows that having to wait for a machine to heat up is more than anyone can bear. Far better to get yourself a good, old-fashioned sandwich toaster that you place directly over the heat. Then go get some of the kids' chocolate to put in your sandwiches. Chocolate + regression + guilt = yum-yum!

**Serves 2 (or 1 in the event of a really big bout of the blues)**
**Preparation and cooking time: 2 minutes (and not a minute more, I promise!)**

an old-fashioned sandwich toaster (a small frying pan can also be used)

4 slices brioche
1 bar of chocolate or a jar of chocolate spread
a little butter

Butter the brioche slices, then place them, buttered-side down, on the sandwich toaster or in the frying pan. Slice the chocolate bar or spread the chocolate spread on one of the brioche slices. Place the other slice on top and toast until a delicious aroma pervades your kitchen, then enjoy!

# Marshmallow and White Chocolate Squares

**Serves 10–12**
**Preparation time: 15 minutes**
**Cooling time: 1 hour**

1 jelly-roll pan or rectangular gratin dish

½ cup unsalted butter, melted and cooled again
2 cups crushed butter cookies
1⅓ cups grated coconut
14-ounce can sweetened condensed milk
2 cups miniature marshmallows
5 ounces white chocolate

Mix together all the ingredients except the marshmallows and chocolate and spread out in a jelly-roll pan. Place in a refrigerator.

Sprinkle the marshmallows over the cookie mixture. Melt the white chocolate and spread over the marshmallows. Leave to cool for about 1 hour, preferably not in a refrigerator, as the humidity may spoil the chocolate.

Marshmallow and White Chocolate Squares

# Nanaimo Bars

These bars are named after the town in British Columbia, Canada, where they are said to have originated. I often include these little cakes cut into small squares in an "all chocolate" selection for dessert. This is a recipe that really calls for English custard powder, but if you can't find any, just add a few drops of vanilla extract and add 2½ tablespoons sugar at this stage of the recipe.

**Serves 8–10**
**Preparation time: 20 minutes**
**Chilling time: 2½ hours**

1 jelly-roll pan or 1 rectangular gratin dish
1 handheld electric mixer

**First layer**
4 ounces best-quality dark chocolate
½ cup unsalted butter
¼ cup sugar
1 egg, beaten
3 teaspoons cocoa powder
2½ cups crushed graham crackers
⅔ cup grated coconut
½ cup walnuts or pecans, chopped

**Second layer**
¼ cup unsalted butter, softened
2¼ cups confectioners' sugar
3 tablespoons custard powder (see above)
3–4 tablespoons water

**Third layer**
¼ cup unsalted butter, softened
3 ounces best-quality dark chocolate
½ cup confectioners' sugar

For the first layer, melt the chocolate, butter, and sugar in a microwave oven or in a bowl over hot water. Add the beaten egg and heat gently, but do not allow to boil. Remove from the heat and incorporate the remaining ingredients.

Transfer this mixture to a jelly-roll pan or a gratin dish and spread out into a layer about ½ inch thick. Place in a refrigerator for 1 hour.

Using an electric mixer, beat together all the ingredients for the second layer until the mixture is smooth. Spread this mixture over the first layer once it has chilled and return to the refrigerator for about 30 minutes.

For the third layer, slowly melt the butter and chocolate in a microwave oven or in a bowl over hot water. Combine with the confectioners' sugar and spread over the first two layers once they have chilled. Place in a refrigerator for about 1 hour before cutting into squares.

## Cookie Hearts

**Makes about 10**
**Preparation time: 15 minutes**
**Cooking time: 15 minutes**
**Decoration: 20 minutes**

1 heart-shaped cookie cutter
1 cookie sheet
brown paper bag
1 pastry wheel (or 1 pair of scissors)

1 cup plus 2 tablespoons very cold salted butter,
chopped into small pieces
⅜ cup sugar
2⅔ cups all-purpose flour
cocoa powder to decorate

Preheat the oven to 300°F.

Using your fingers or a food processor, work
together all the ingredients until the mixture
resembles fine breadcrumbs. Knead for 1 minute
on a cold, lightly floured surface. Roll the dough
out with a rolling pin and cut into heart shapes.
Place on a cookie sheet and bake for about
15 minutes or until the cookies are golden
on top.

Cut out paper stencils for various messages (such
as "Love" or someone's name), place on top of
the cookies, and sprinkle with the cocoa powder.

## Painting in Chocolate

**To cover about 1 square yard**
**Preparation time: 2 minutes**
**Cooling time: 5 minutes**

4 ounces dark chocolate
¼ cup unsalted butter
2 tablespoons water

Melt the ingredients together in a microwave
oven or in a bowl over hot water. Leave to cool
before doing whatever you want with this
chocolate "paint."

*Chocolate cocktails*

# Smooth and Creamy

2¼ cups milk
2 ounces best-quality dark chocolate, cut into small pieces
1 egg yolk
½ cup rum or brandy

Heat the milk and pour it over the chocolate, stirring until it melts completely. Leave to cool in a refrigerator. Transfer the chocolate milk to a cocktail shaker or blender and combine with the egg yolk and alcohol.

## Variations

Add 1 tablespoon sugar, 3 tablespoons fresh orange juice, and 1 small glass Grand Marnier to the chocolate milk.

Alternatively, add 2 tablespoons honey, the grated rind of 1 lemon, ½ glass of rum, ½ teaspoon ground ginger, and ½ teaspoon five-spice powder.

# Brandy Alexandra

4 parts light cream
3 parts brandy
3 parts chocolate liqueur
cocoa powder or grated nutmeg to decorate

Place the liquid ingredients in a cocktail shaker or large container and stir or shake well. Sprinkle with the cocoa powder or nutmeg. A perfect cocktail to round off an evening.

# Sausage

The ladies at the coffee get-togethers in Ireland, whom I mentioned earlier, clearly never intended this name for their recipe, but my French tasting panel thought the result looked so much like a sausage that the name stuck.

**Makes about 20 slices**
**Preparation time: 15 minutes**
**Chilling time: 7 hours**

plastic wrap

4 ounces best-quality dark chocolate
¼ cup unsalted butter
1¼ cups hazelnuts, coarsely crushed
12 soft, fruit-filled cookies, cut into quarters
¾ cup golden raisins
2–3 teaspoons confectioners' sugar

Melt the chocolate and butter in a microwave oven or in a bowl over hot water. Add all the remaining ingredients and stir well.

Chill briefly in a refrigerator. When the mixture has cooled sufficiently to not stick to the hands, roll it into a sausage shape.

Chill for at least 6–7 hours.

Coat in the confectioners' sugar and cut into slices.

SUGGESTION • Enjoy with a glass of sweet or fortified red wine such as Banyls or Maury. The original recipe includes 3 tablespoons of brandy or amaretto. If made with the alcohol, you can serve the Sausage with coffee at the end of a meal.

Sausage

# Triple Chocolate Brownie Crunch

I know, I know, it really is over the top . . . but you can always say "no" to a second helping!

**Serves 8**
**Total preparation time: 30 minutes**
**Chilling time: 3 hours**

## The white chocolate mousse layer

**Preparation time: 5 minutes**
**Chilling time: 3 hours**

1 saucepan
1 handheld electric mixer

¾ cup whipping cream
8 ounces white chocolate, finely chopped

Heat the cream and pour it over the chocolate. Stir well until the chocolate has melted. The mixture should be smooth and glossy. Leave to cool for 1 hour, then beat with an electric mixer.

## The brownie layer

**Preparation time: 10 minutes**
**Cooking time: 30 minutes**

1 square or rectangular baking pan

6 tablespoons unsalted butter
4 ounces best-quality dark chocolate
2 eggs, beaten
1 cup sugar
⅔ cup all-purpose flour
½ cup toasted, crushed hazelnuts, macadamia nuts, or pecans

Preheat the oven to 350°F.

Grease an 8-inch-square baking pan or a rectangular gratin dish of approximately the same size.

Melt the butter and chocolate in a microwave oven or in a bowl over hot water. Add the beaten eggs, followed by the sugar and flour. Stir quickly but gently, then incorporate the crushed nuts you've chosen. Transfer to the baking pan and bake for about 30 minutes. The cake should be crisp on top and soft inside.

## The milk chocolate sauce

**Preparation time: 5 minutes**

1 saucepan

scant 1 cup light cream
½ cup milk
5 ounces milk chocolate, finely chopped

Bring the cream and milk to a boil. Pour the mixture over the chocolate and stir well. Serve hot or allow to cool.

## To assemble

When the brownie has cooled completely, spread with a layer of white chocolate mousse and leave to chill in a refrigerator for at least 2–3 hours.

To serve, cut the brownie into squares and top with the milk chocolate sauce. Chop one of your favorite chocolate bars into small pieces and sprinkle on top.

## Rich Milk Chocolate, Date, and Almond Cake

A delicious cake in which the sweet taste of the milk chocolate blends with that of the dates and almonds. You could use hazelnuts instead of the almonds for even more flavor.

**Serves 8–10**
**Preparation time: 15 minutes**
**Cooking time: 50 minutes**

1 shallow cake pan, 10 inches in diameter
1 handheld electric mixer
waxed paper

¾ cup unsalted butter
9 ounces good-quality milk chocolate
3 whole eggs
3 egg yolks
⅔ cup light brown sugar
2 cups ground almonds
¾ cup whole almonds, toasted and crushed
1 cup medjool dates, chopped (if you can't find any, poach some dates in water and sugar for 3 minutes)

Grease the baking pan and line the base with a circle of greased waxed paper.

Preheat the oven to 325°F.

Melt the butter and chocolate in a microwave oven or in a bowl over hot water. Beat the three whole eggs with the egg yolks and sugar until the mixture is pale and thick. Add the ground almonds, crushed almonds, and dates and combine well. Incorporate the butter and chocolate mixture. Pour into the baking pan and bake for about 50 minutes.

Leave to cool before turning out.

Serve with sour cream and a sprinkling of milk chocolate shavings. *LASALLETTE*
*Labour Day Weekend 2012*
*excellent - careful not to*
*overcook!*

## Hazelnut and White Chocolate Cake

**Serves 6–8**
**Preparation time: 15 minutes**
**Cooking time: 30 minutes**

1 8-inch-square baking pan
1 hand whisk

5 egg whites
1 cup ground hazelnuts
⅔ cup sugar
½ cup all-purpose flour
½ cup salted butter, melted
a few pecans to decorate
4 ounces white chocolate

Preheat the oven to 400°F.

Whisk the egg whites into stiff peaks. Add the hazelnuts and sugar and fold in gently. Add the flour, then the butter.

Transfer the mixture to a greased baking pan and bake for 15 minutes.

Reduce the temperature to 300°F and bake for another 10 minutes.

Remove from the oven, leave to cool slightly before turning out, then leave to cool completely.

Arrange the pecans over the top of the cake. Melt the chocolate, then pour it over the cake and pecans. Leave to set before serving.

Rich Milk Chocolate, Date, and Almond Cake

Chocolate for kid.

The Good Old Chocolate Sandwich

I know that most people make no distinction between food for children and food for adults, but I have devoted a separate chapter to children for the following reasons:

1 To the best of my knowledge, there are not many adults who meet up on weekend afternoons to blow out the candles on their birthday cakes in a celebration of sugar.

2 Most of these recipes really can be made *by* the children, or at least with their active participation. That way, they get twice as much pleasure, as the best part is licking the bowl clean. And what's more, the pediatricians will be impressed by their progress in motivation, newfound tastes, logic, and social skills.

3 I have tried out all the recipes on my own children, their cousins, and their friends at real parties and snack time. They love them.

4 Almost all of the recipes in this chapter are ideas for special moments. These are not simply after-school snacks, except perhaps the Good Old Chocolate Sandwich, which goes down well with a large glass of milk!

If, in spite of everything, you find there is just a bit too much sugar, do what I do: Throw out the calorie-loaded, vitamin-poor soft drinks and give them fruit juice and milk with some of these treats.

## The Good Old Chocolate Sandwich

Not so much a recipe as a flashback to our childhood days.

Served with a large glass of milk, there's no beating this quick-to-make after-school snack. Obviously, most nutritionists prefer this type of snack to excessively sugary cakes washed down with soft drinks. The only snag is finding the time and a parking space by the bakery when you go to buy the fresh bread.

CHILDREN ARE NOT THE LEAST BIT BOTHERED ABOUT BEING COOL AND TRENDY when it comes to finding their favorite candies, chocolate bars, and cereals in cakes. Give such creations a slightly funny name, and party food immediately becomes magic.

# Sleeping Teddies

Watch out! This recipe goes down extremely well with everybody, so double the quantities if there are adults around, too!

**Makes 12**
**Preparation time: 15 minutes**
**Cooling time: 45 minutes**

12 baking cups, 1½–2 inches in diameter

5 ounces chocolate (dark, white, or milk)
4–5 handfuls of any breakfast cereal you happen to have in your cupboard
12 chocolate teddy bears
(preferably round, fat ones!)

Melt the chocolate and combine it with the cereal. Place a teaspoonful of the mixture in each muffin cup and flatten it slightly before topping with a teddy bear, face up. Leave the chocolate to set.

# Top Hats

In my childhood, no birthday party was complete without these little fancies.

**Makes 20**
**Preparation time: 30 minutes, including cooling**

20 small baking cups

11 ounces dark or milk chocolate
20 colored, candy-coated chocolate pieces
20 marshmallows

Melt the chocolate in a microwave oven or in a bowl over hot water. Pour a teaspoonful in each muffin cup and top with a marshmallow, pressing down slightly so the chocolate comes about halfway up the marshmallow.

Place a drop of chocolate on each marshmallow and top with a little candy-coated chocolate. Leave to cool.

# Homemade Chocolate Bars

This is a culinary activity that children really love. A quick, fun, and delicious recipe for children of all ages.

2 or 3 sheets of waxed paper
spatulas for spreading chocolate
1 mixing bowl and 1 spoon per child

**Dark, milk, or white chocolate (4–5 ounces per child); try to find couverture chocolate, which melts very easily**
**all sorts of packaged chocolate candies (they come in all sizes nowadays)**
**hazelnuts and raisins**
**puffed rice cereal**

It is essential to work on a cold, smooth surface. If you do not have any tiles or a cold work surface in your kitchen, look for some small, inexpensive metal trays. The room should be cool (maximum 64–66°F).

If you value the friendship of your guests' parents, you will also need aprons or shirts that can withstand anything.

Then all they have to do is melt the chocolate, add the ingredient(s) of their choice, spread the mixture out on a sheet of waxed paper, put in a cool place, and wait a half hour for the chocolate to set.

If you have opted to work on small trays, you can slip them in a refrigerator, then the children can eat their creations sooner!

Have little bags ready in the unlikely event that they have some left to take home with them.

Tim - age 6
Milk chocolate + cereal

Corentin - age 9
Milk chocolate + chocolate candies

Camille - age 10
Dark chocolate + hazelnuts

Tanguy - age 5
White chocolate and chocolate candies

Chocolate for kids 105

# Rice Cereal Tower

This is a "cake" that's quick and fun to make. Buy some long candles to give it a festive feel.

**Serves 10–12**
**Preparation time: 30 minutes**
**Cooling and assembling time: 30 minutes**

4 sheets of waxed paper
a marble slab or cold, smooth surface

9 ounces dark chocolate
5 ounces white chocolate
5 ounces milk chocolate
13-ounce box puffed rice cereal

Melt the different types of chocolate separately in a microwave oven or in a bowl over hot water, using only 7 ounces of the dark chocolate.

For the base, combine the melted dark chocolate with slightly more than a third of the puffed rice in a mixing bowl. Spoon onto a sheet of waxed paper and shape into a disk about 8 inches in diameter. Smooth well.

Divide the remaining cereal between the remaining two types of chocolate and stir gently. On the remaining three sheets of waxed paper, place disks of each type of chocolate measuring 3–3½ inches in diameter. Leave in a cool place to set.

When the pieces have set, melt the remaining dark chocolate; it will act as glue. Assemble the cake, using the 8-inch disk as the base, alternating the different types of chocolate. Secure the candles with the melted chocolate and leave to set completely.

# Fingerprints

A recipe especially for modeling-clay fanatics.

## The cookies

**Makes about 36**
**Preparation time: 45 minutes**
**Cooking time: about 15 minutes**

2 cookie sheets
1 handheld electric mixer

¼ cup unsalted butter, softened
⅔ cup soft brown sugar
1 tablespoon milk
1½ cups all-purpose flour

Preheat the oven to 350°F.

Cream the butter with the sugar using the electric mixer. Add the milk and beat until the mixture is smooth. Incorporate the flour, then knead with your hands to form a soft dough.

Divide the dough into three and roll into sausage shapes 1 inch in diameter. Cut each sausage into twelve pieces.

Roll each piece between your hands to form a ball. Place the balls on two cookie sheets. Press your thumb down on each of them to form a small hollow.

Bake for about 15 minutes until the cookies are golden. Remove from the oven and leave to cool.

## The glaze

**4 ounces dark, white, or milk chocolate, according to taste**
**5 tablespoons unsalted butter**

Melt the chocolate and butter in a microwave oven or in a bowl over hot water.

Using a teaspoon, place a drop of glaze in the hollow in each cookie and leave to set before serving.

1 2
3 4
5 6

Chocolate for kids     Butterfly Cupcakes

Jean-François's Stuck Cake

# Butterfly Cupcakes

**Makes about 20**
**Preparation time: 30 minutes**
**Cooking time: 15 minutes**

1 handheld electric mixer
20 baking cups
1 muffin pan

½ cup unsalted butter, softened
½ cup sugar
3 eggs
scant 1 cup all-purpose flour
3½ tablespoons cocoa powder
1½ teaspoons baking powder

**Butter cream**
14 tablespoons (1¾ sticks) unsalted butter, softened
3 cups confectioners' sugar
6 tablespoons cocoa powder, dissolved in
2 tablespoons hot water

Preheat the oven to 375°F.

Place the baking cups in the muffin pan.

Place all the ingredients in a mixing bowl and beat with an electric mixer for 2–3 minutes, until the mixture is smooth. Half-fill the baking cups and bake for about 15 minutes. The cupcakes should be well risen on top and soft to the touch.

Remove from the oven and leave to cool completely.

Now make the butter cream. Using the electric mixer, cream the ingredients together until the mixture is light and fluffy. Cut out a circle from the top of each bun, leaving a hollow; cut each circle in half. Place a little butter cream in each hollow, then insert the two lid halves at an angle to resemble butterfly wings.

Sprinkle with confectioners' sugar and serve.

# Jean-François's Stuck Cake

At nursery school, Jean-François was in love with Virginie. She, on the other hand, a chocoholic even at that tender age, loved him mainly for the chocolate cake his grandmother gave them after school. As soon as she got the recipe from his grandma, she dumped the poor boy. But the tale has a happy ending, because we still have the recipe today! This cake is a delight, and the fact that it is impossible to turn out means you need have no worries about presentation or decorum. It's not often you have the chance to encourage everyone to dive into a dish all at once!

**Serves 8–10**
**Preparation time: 10 minutes**
**Cooking time: 20 minutes**

1 shallow cake pan, about 12 inches in diameter

9 ounces chocolate
1 cups plus 2 tablespoons unsalted butter
6 eggs, separated
1¼ cups sugar

Preheat the oven to 350°F.

Melt the chocolate and butter in a microwave oven or in a bowl over hot water. Beat the egg yolks and the sugar until the mixture is pale. Combine the two mixtures. Whisk the egg whites into stiff peaks and fold them into the chocolate mixture. Pour into the cake pan and bake for about 20 minutes. The cake will rise, then collapse again, leaving a raised crust around the edges. Serve in the pan, still warm if you are eager to dive in!

# Sorbet and Ice-Cream Chocolate Cups

More of a trick than a recipe, these little sorbets are great for parties and birthday meals because you can prepare them in advance and store them in your freezer. What's more, they do away with the need for cutlery and plates. You can buy the chocolate cups from good delicatessens and major supermarkets.

Alternatively, you can make your own. Just coat the inside of baking cups with good-quality melted chocolate using a brush. Leave the chocolate in a cool place to set before adding the ice cream or sorbet.

Sorbet and Ice-Cream Chocolate Cups

# Chocolate Marquise

I have included this recipe in the children's section because of the marchioness decoration (*marquise* in French), perfect for a young girl's birthday cake. However, many children do not like desserts that are so rich in butter and cream. If that is the case with your family, just make the marchioness's full skirt with a selection of different ice creams. Decorate it with chocolate and/or fresh fruit and serve with little cupcakes or cookies.

**Serves 8–10**
**Preparation time: 20 minutes**
**Chilling time: overnight**

1 deep baking pan
1 confectioner's decorative model (available from trade suppliers or specialty cookware stores)
plastic wrap

## The cake

11 ounces best-quality dark chocolate
¾ cup unsalted butter, softened
½ cup superfine sugar
4 eggs, separated

## The chantilly cream

1 cup whipping cream
3 tablespoons confectioners' sugar

Melt the chocolate in a microwave oven or in a bowl over hot water.

Cream the butter with the sugar until the mixture is light and fluffy, then add the chocolate and the egg yolks. Whisk the egg whites into stiff peaks and fold into the chocolate mixture in three batches so that they do not collapse.

Pour the mixture into the baking pan lined with plastic wrap and leave to chill overnight in a refrigerator.

The next day, whip the cream until it forms soft peaks, then add the confectioners' sugar, continuing to beat until the cream is very stiff.

Turn the chocolate marquise out onto a serving dish and place the confectioner's model on top. Spread the chantilly cream over the cake and decorate her full skirt any way you want—for example, you could use chocolate shavings.

# Snowy Forest Cake

A festive cake that is quite tricky to make, but the result is clearly worth the effort! Perfect for that winter birthday.

**Preparation time: 40 minutes**
**Cooking time: 25 minutes**

2 shallow cake pans, 9 inches in diameter
1 electric mixer
1 sheet of waxed paper

1 cup whipping cream
4½ ounces white chocolate
½ cup unsalted butter, softened
¾ cup sugar
3 eggs
2 cups all-purpose flour
2 teaspoons baking powder

**Filling and frosting**
1½ cups unsalted butter
7 cups sifted confectioners' sugar, plus
1 tablespoon for decoration
1½ cups lemon curd or pudding
1 white or transparent ribbon

Preheat the oven to 350°F.

Grease the cake pans and line the bases with circles of waxed paper.

Heat the cream and pour it over the chocolate, stirring well. Using the electric mixer, cream the butter with the sugar for 3–4 minutes, until the mixture is light and fluffy. Add the eggs one by one, stirring constantly. Then add the flour and the baking powder, and the chocolate mixture alternately, beating briefly after each addition.

Pour the mixture into the pans and bake for 20–25 minutes.

Leave to cool in the pans for 10 minutes, then turn out onto a wire rack. Peel off the waxed paper and leave to cool completely.

When the cakes are completely cooled, cut them in half horizontally to produce four layers.

To make the butter cream, cream the butter with the confectioners' sugar until the mixture is light and fluffy.

Assemble the cake, spreading a quarter of the butter cream on the first layer, followed by a thin layer of lemon curd or pudding. Place the second layer of cake on top and repeat the procedure. Repeat again with the third layer of cake, then top with the fourth and final layer.

Spread with a final layer of lemon curd, then cover the whole cake with the butter cream.

Using a fork, make snowy peaks in the frosting.

## The forest and pine trees

To make the forest, draw pine trees on a sheet of white paper with a dark felt pen. Melt 4 ounces white chocolate in a microwave oven or in a bowl over hot water. Place a sheet of waxed paper over the drawing paper. Using a brush, paint the chocolate over the pine tree shapes. Leave in a cool place for 1–2 hours to set completely.

Another solution, a bit more freestyle, is to simply draw the pine trees directly onto the sheet of waxed paper freehand, with no pattern (as in the photograph). It's up to you to decide, as you are the best judge of your painting skills!

## The snow

Before serving, dredge with confectioners' sugar and run a ribbon around the cake.

TIP • If you really can't cope with the idea of making the chocolate pine trees, just forget them: Go straight to the last section and simply call it "snow-scene cake."

# Chic chocolate

To round off a good meal, once the hunger pangs have been vanquished and the taste buds tickled, I need much more subtle combinations and flavors. This is when spices, fruits, contrasts in texture and temperature, presentation, and, above all, the quality of the chocolate play an even greater role. I am very picky. If it's not absolutely top quality, this is the only time I can imagine not leaving a clean plate. And I'll be dwelling on it all through the following day . . .

Chocolate can be cruel!

Baileys Cream Pots

# Dips

Often, after a substantial appetizer and main course, you don't want a large dessert—just a few mouthfuls of something sweet. Appetizers tempt the appetite before the meal. These little creations are more appetizers to tickle the sweet taste buds. And now it's up to you to discover other variations on a chocolate theme; other associations of flavors, colors, and textures depending on your own personal taste, the season, and what you have in your cupboards. If you do not have any little liquor glasses, use coffee cups instead. I have not specified any quantities because they are very difficult to calculate for such tiny morsels and depend on the size of your glasses or cups.

## Milk chocolate ganache, marrons glacés, and sour cream

To make the ganache, use equal quantities of chocolate and whipping cream. Heat the cream, pour it over the chocolate, stir, and pour into glasses or cups. Leave to cool before sprinkling with the crumbled marrons glacés, and top with a dollop of sour cream to give a hint of acidity.

## Pureed prunes with Armagnac, mascarpone cheese, and dark chocolate

If you cannot find any prune puree, poach the prunes in a little water for a minute or two and process in a blender. Add a little Armagnac and pour some of this mixture into each glass or cup.

Beat the mascarpone until smooth, then spread a layer over the pureed prunes. Top with dark chocolate shavings.

## Rhubarb, white chocolate mousse, and crushed ladyfingers

Poach the rhubarb in a little water and sugar. When it is soft, crush it with a fork and pour into glasses or cups. Make a mousse using the recipe on page 20 and pour a little over the rhubarb compote. Top with crushed ladyfingers, or to be extra chic, try to find some really interesting little cookies in a specialty store. Serve with chocolate snacks of your choice that are suitable for dipping and provide long-handled spoons so as not to waste a drop.

# Baileys Cream Pots

**Serves 6–8**
**Preparation time: 5 minutes**
**Chilling time: 1 hour**

1 handheld electric mixer
6–8 small bowls or ramekins

7 ounces best-quality dark chocolate
1 cup whipping cream
¼ cup mascarpone cheese
5 tablespoons Baileys
chocolate shavings to decorate

Melt the chocolate in a microwave oven or in a bowl over hot water.

Whip the cream with the mascarpone, then stir in the Baileys.

Pour the cream mixture into individual serving dishes. Pour the melted chocolate over the cream mixture, stirring with a small spoon to create a marbled effect, then decorate with the chocolate shavings and chill in a refrigerator for 1 hour before serving.

# Granola Tuiles and Coffee Granita

**Serves 6**
**Preparation time: 5 minutes**
**Chilling time: 4 hours**

1 freezer container
1 sheet of waxed paper

**Tuiles**
7 ounces best-quality dark chocolate
granola (see recipe on page 86)

**Granita**
heaping ½ cup sugar
2¾ cups very strong espresso coffee

Dissolve the sugar in the coffee and leave to cool completely before transferring the mixture to a freezer container and placing it in a freezer. Using a fork, stir the frozen granita around the edges into the unfrozen, every hour for five hours, to create an even mixture.

Melt the chocolate and spoon it onto the sheet of waxed paper to form circular but irregular shapes about 4 inches in diameter. Sprinkle a few spoonfuls of granola on top and leave to set.

Serve with the granita.

Excellent sorbets are available at supermarkets if you do not have time to make the granita.

Granola Tuiles and Coffee Granita

# "I Made it Myself" Cake with Berries

The chocolate casing takes a bit of skill. But if it's a really important occasion or you're out to impress, this dessert is just the one.

**Serves 12**
**About 2 hours in total**

## The cake

**Preparation time: 5 minutes**
**Cooking time: 25 minutes**

1 electric mixer or food processor
2 shallow, round cake pans, 8 inches in diameter

1 cup unsalted butter or margarine, softened
1 cup sugar
4 eggs
2 cups all-purpose flour
3 tablespoons cocoa powder combined with
3 tablespoons hot water
2 teaspoons baking powder

Preheat the oven to 350°F.

Grease and line the two cake pans.

Place all the ingredients in a mixing bowl and beat using the electric mixer until the mixture is very smooth. Transfer the mixture to the cake pans and bake for 25 minutes.

The top of the cake should be soft to the touch.

Remove from the oven, leave to cool for a few minutes in the pans, then turn out onto a wire rack to cool completely.

## The ganache

**Preparation time: 5 minutes**
**Chilling time: 10 minutes**

1 saucepan
1 handheld electric mixer

1½ cups whipping cream
12 ounces best-quality dark chocolate, cut into small pieces

Bring the cream almost to a boil and pour it over the chocolate; the cream will melt the chocolate. Stir well until the mixture is smooth and glossy.

Beat with the electric mixer until the mixture attains a mousse-like consistency and has cooled completely.

Cut the cakes in half horizontally to make four disk layers. Spread some of the ganache on one disk layer and place the second disk layer on top. Repeat this procedure with the third and fourth layers, then decorate the top of the cake with the remaining ganache. Place in a refrigerator to chill.

## The casing and decoration

**Preparation time: 10 minutes**

2 sheets of waxed paper
1 friend to help with the chocolate casing

7 ounces best-quality dark chocolate
3 cups mixed berries

Work in a dry and cool room (64–66°F).

Using a ruler, measure the height of the cake.

From one of the sheets of waxed paper, cut out a strip as wide as the cake is high and a little longer than the circumference of the cake.

Place the uncut sheet of waxed paper on a marble pastry slab or other smooth, cold surface to catch any excess chocolate, and lay the cutout strip on top.

Melt the chocolate in a microwave oven or in a bowl over hot water. Pour the melted chocolate over the strip and spread evenly using the spatula. Leave the chocolate to cool until it has set slightly. It should no longer be liquid, but it should still be flexible enough to bend to the shape of the cake. Take the strip and attach it, chocolate side toward the cake, pressing down lightly. An extra pair of hands is useful here.

Decorate the top of the cake with seasonal berries of your choice.

Place the cake in the refrigerator. Remove from the refrigerator about 20 minutes before serving, but do not peel off the strip of waxed paper until just before serving.

# Chocolate Roulade

I think this dessert is one of the most difficult to make successfully. It's not the preparation or the cooking that presents problems, but the rolling-up technique at the end. You are bound to be more dextrous than I am, but read the instructions carefully anyway—don't miss anything! You will find the result well worth the effort. Once you have mastered the knack, you can combine this wonderful dessert with a whole host of delicious cream fillings, sauces, and crispy additions.

**Serves 8**
**Preparation time: 25 minutes**
**Cooking time: 20 minutes**

1 jelly-roll pan
waxed paper
1 handheld electric mixer

6 ounces best-quality dark chocolate, in chips or broken into small pieces
5 eggs, separated
¾ cup sugar
2 tablespoons confectioners' sugar
2 tablespoons cocoa powder

Preheat the oven to 350°F.

Place the waxed paper over the base of the jelly-roll pan.

Melt the chocolate in a microwave oven or in a bowl over hot water.

Beat the egg yolks with the sugar until the mixture is pale and frothy. Fold in the slightly cooled melted chocolate.

Whisk the egg whites into soft peaks and fold into the chocolate mixture in three batches so that the egg whites do not collapse.

Spread the mixture over the base of the jelly-roll pan and smooth out evenly. Bake for 15–20 minutes or until the cake is firm on top but still soft to the touch.

Remove from the oven, place a second sheet of waxed paper over the hot cake, and leave to cool.

Once the cake has cooled, carefully remove the waxed paper from the cake, place the paper clean-side up on a work surface, and sprinkle it with the confectioners' sugar and baking cocoa.

Very carefully—summon some assistance if you can—turn out the cake onto the waxed paper that has been sprinkled with sugar and cocoa.

Peel off the sheet of waxed paper used to line the pan—do this very carefully, as well.

If you want your roulade to have straight edges, neaten them now by cutting in a straight line along the edges.

Spread the roulade filling over the cake, leaving 1 inch at the top, and taking care not to add too much filling.

Start to roll up the cake using the sheet of waxed paper beneath the cake. It is essential that the first roll is very tight (1 inch in diameter), to give a real jelly-roll effect. Don't worry if the cake cracks in places; it looks better and more appetizing that way.

You can keep the paper wrapped tightly around the roulade and leave it to cool with its filling to help it hold its shape, removing the paper just before serving.

## The filling

Choose any recipe from the "Tool Kit" section.

# Chocolate Quenelles

**Serves 8**
**Preparation time: 15 minutes**
**Chilling time: 8 hours**

1 saucepan
1 handheld electric mixer

**4 egg yolks**
**½ cup superfine sugar**
**½ cup milk**
**1 cup whipping cream**
**8 ounces best-quality dark chocolate**

Beat the egg yolks with the sugar until the mixture is pale and fluffy. Heat the milk with the cream, pour it over the egg yolks, then cook (in the same way as a custard).

When the mixture thickens, pour it over the chocolate, stirring constantly.

Cover and chill overnight in the refrigerator.

Shape into quenelles using two tablespoons and serve with fresh fruit.

TIP • If you find making the custard mixture too daunting a prospect, quenelles can also be made with ganache:

Pour 1 cup very hot whipping cream over 8 ounces chocolate and stir well until the mixture is smooth and creamy. Chill overnight in the refrigerator before serving.

Baked Pear with a Chocolate Pesto Filling

Emmanuelle's Chocolate Cookie Cake

# Baked Pear with a Chocolate Pesto Filling

**Serves 4**
**Preparation time: 5 minutes**
**Cooking time: 15 minutes**

1 coffee grinder

4 firm, fresh pears
¼ cup finely chopped nuts
¼ cup finely chopped apricots or raisins
4 teaspoons honey
¼ cup dark chocolate chips
¼ cup salted butter

Preheat the oven to 350°F.

Slice the tops from the pears, setting them aside for the lids. Scoop out the core and the seeds.

Combine all the ingredients, apart from the butter, to form a thick dough.

Fill the pears to overflowing, place a pat of butter on this "pesto," top with the "lid," and bake for about 15 minutes. Serve hot with vanilla ice cream.

# White Chocolate and Raspberry Mille-feuille

**Serves 4**
**Preparation time: 30 minutes**

1 electric mixer
1 sheet of waxed paper
1 pastry bag

11 ounces white chocolate
½ cup whipping cream
3½ cups fresh raspberries
2–3 tablespoons confectioners' sugar

Melt 7 ounces of the chocolate and shape into twelve rectangles (or circles) on the waxed paper. Leave to cool.

Melt the remaining chocolate and leave to cool slightly. Meanwhile, whip the cream, then fold in the chocolate to form a mousse, and transfer the mixture to the pastry bag.

To assemble the mille-feuille, place one layer of cooled chocolate on the serving dish, then pipe out a layer of mousse. Place a second piece of chocolate on top, pressing down slightly so that it adheres to the creamy mousse filling. Then arrange the raspberries on the chocolate. Top with the remaining layer of chocolate, using a smear of mousse to secure the fruit.

Dredge with confectioners' sugar before serving.

# Emmanuelle's Chocolate Cookie Cake

The key ingredient of this cake, which is a real favorite with the children, also meets with the wholehearted approval of adults. Best when cut in very thin slices.

**Serves 8**
**Preparation time: 15 minutes**
**Chilling time: 12 hours**

1 saucepan
1 loaf pan
plastic wrap

12 ounces plain butter cookies
2 ounces meringue cookies
4 ounces dark chocolate
1½ cups unsalted butter
2 eggs, lightly beaten
heaping ½ cup sugar
½ cup cocoa powder

Break the cookies into small pieces by hand. It is important that they do not disintegrate into powdery crumbs; they should be uneven pieces measuring about ½ inch.

Melt the chocolate with the butter in a microwave oven or in a bowl over hot water, and leave to cool. Add the eggs, sugar, and cocoa powder and stir well.

Line the loaf pan with plastic wrap and add the mixture, pressing it down slightly. Chill in a refrigerator for at least 6 hours or preferably overnight. Serve with whipped cream or any other topping of your choice.

TIP • I have adapted Emmanuelle's recipe slightly. Originally the only chocolate ingredient it contained was about ¾ cup cocoa powder. I prefer to blend it with melted dark chocolate to create a moister and slightly less strongly flavored cake. Why not give them both a try? The advantage of Emmanuelle's version is that it doesn't need a saucepan!

White Chocolate and Raspberry Mille-feuille

# Chocolate Sorbet with Preserved Ginger, Orange, and Sesame Caramel

Disorganized by nature, especially at the end of a meal, I have shied away from using my ice-cream machine for a year now, preferring to buy delicious ice-cream desserts from a good ice-cream shop. This very easy recipe was devised at the River Café in London, England. It certainly helped me overcome my reluctance and made me feel at ease with this diabolic machine, which so far has made either iced soup or sweet ice cubes. Apparently all you have to do is tame it. I'll master it one day!

**Serves 6–8**
**Preparation time: 10 minutes**
**Cooking time: 20 minutes**

1 ice-cream machine
2 saucepans, one of which should be heavy-based (for the caramel)
1 marble pastry slab

## The sorbet

2¾ cups mineral water
1 generous cup superfine sugar
1½ cups cocoa powder
½ glass Vecchia Romagna liqueur (or brandy, Armagnac, or dark rum)

Boil the water with the sugar for 5 minutes. Add the cocoa powder, stir, and cook over a low heat for 15 minutes, stirring constantly. Leave to cool.

Add the alcohol, then follow the instructions for the ice-cream machine.

## The decoration

3 strips candied orange peel
1 tablespoon finely chopped preserved ginger
2 tablespoons sesame seeds

Toast the sesame seeds in a saucepan or bake on a cookie sheet for 1 or 2 minutes in an oven preheated to 350°F.

Combine the sesame seeds with the preserved fruits and spoon into small mounds on the marble slab.

## The caramel
## (at least I can make that!)

½ cup sugar

To make the caramel, melt the sugar very gently in a heavy-based saucepan, then pour it over the sesame seeds and preserved fruits, making them into attractively irregular shapes. Leave to cool. To serve, scoop balls of the sorbet into a glass and insert pieces of caramel.

TIP • If you do not have an ice-cream machine, which I would quite understand, you can opt for a much simpler version of this recipe: Just buy a good-quality chocolate sorbet from an ice-cream shop or supermarket.

# Dacquoise Meringue with Chocolate Cream and Caramelized Hazelnuts

**Serves 10–12**
**Preparation time: 40 minutes**
**Cooking time: 1 hour**
**Chilling time: 4 hours**

2 saucepans
1 marble pastry slab
2 cookie sheets
2 sheets of waxed paper
1 pastry bag

**For the dacquoise meringue**
12 egg whites
1½ cups superfine sugar
2 cups ground hazelnuts

**For the chocolate cream filling**
6 egg yolks
¼ cup sugar
2 tablespoons all-purpose flour
1½ cups whipping cream
1½ cups milk
4 ounces best-quality dark chocolate

**For the whipped cream topping**
1½ cups whipping cream
2 tablespoons mascarpone cheese
1 tablespoon sugar

**For the caramelized hazelnuts**
½ cup sugar
3 tablespoons blanched hazelnuts

To make the dacquoise meringue, preheat the oven to 300°F.

Whisk the egg whites into stiff peaks. Add ½ cup sugar and beat until the mixture is glossy. Using a spoon, fold in the remaining sugar, followed by the ground hazelnuts.

Line the cookie sheets with waxed paper, then pipe two disks of the meringue mixture onto each cookie sheet and bake for about 1 hour.

Turn the oven off and leave to cool completely before removing the disks from the oven and peeling off the waxed paper.

To make the chocolate cream filling, beat the egg yolks with the sugar and flour until the mixture is pale and frothy. Bring the cream almost to a boil with the milk and pour it over the mixture. Return the mixture to a boil over a medium heat. When the creamy mixture begins to boil, reduce the heat and cook very gently for 1–2 minutes until it thickens. Stir in the chocolate, leave it to melt, then stir well.

To make the whipped cream topping, whip the cream with the mascarpone and sugar.

To make the caramelized hazelnuts, first make a caramel with the sugar. Place the hazelnuts on the marble pastry slab. Pour the caramel over the nuts and leave to set.

To assemble the dessert, place one meringue disk on a serving dish, then spread with a layer of chocolate cream, followed by a layer of whipped cream. Add a second meringue disk, then repeat this procedure for the remaining disks. Decorate with the caramelized hazelnuts.

TIP • If you don't have a pastry bag, spoon the meringue mixture out in spirals to make more even disks.

# Chocolate, Lime, and Passion Fruit Pavlova

**Serves 8**
**Preparation time: 20 minutes**
**Cooking time: 1 hour**
**Chilling time: 2 hours**

1 handheld electric mixer
waxed paper
1 cookie sheet

## For the meringue

8 egg whites
2 cups soft brown sugar
3 tablespoons cocoa powder
1 teaspoon red wine vinegar

## For the filling

1½ cups whipping cream
2 tablespoons mascarpone cheese (optional)
juice of 5 passion fruits
juice and rind of 1 lime
2 tablespoons sugar

Preheat the oven to 300°F.

Whisk the egg whites into soft peaks with half
the sugar, then gradually add the remaining
sugar, beating constantly. Add the cocoa powder
and vinegar, beating very gently until the mixture
is smooth.

Pour the meringue into a circle on the waxed
paper. Place on the cookie sheet and bake for
1 hour, then turn off the heat and leave to cool
completely in the oven.

Whip the cream with the mascarpone (if using),
then add the passion fruit juice, the juice and
grated rind of the lime, and the sugar.

Spoon the cream mixture into the center of the
meringue. Chill in the refrigerator until you are
ready to serve.